INVALUABLE LESSONS FROM A FROG
Seven Life-Enhancing Metaphors

OLIVIER CLERC

INVALUABLE LESSONS FROM A FROG

Seven Life-Enhancing Metaphors

Translated by Louis Marcelin-Rice

Dreamriver Press

Dreamriver Press LLC
www.dreamriverpress.com
or contact at:
12 Franklin Avenue
Flourtown, PA 19031-2006
U.S.A.

Original published in France as
La grenouille qui ne savait pas qu'elle était cuite... et autres leçons de vie
Copyright © 2005 by Editions JC Lattès

ISBN-13: 978-0-9797908-3-6
ISBN-10: 0-9797908-3-2

Library of Congress Control Number: 2009929666

1. OCC019000 BODY, MIND & SPIRIT / Inspiration & Personal Growth
2. SEL031000   SELF-HELP / Personal Growth / General

Designed by George D. Matthiopoulos

This book is printed on 100% recycled paper.

Preserving our environment
Dreamriver Press chose Legacy Hi-Bulk
Natural 100% post-consumer recycled paper for
the pages of this book printed by Webcom Inc.

Mixed Sources
Product group from well-managed
forests, controlled sources and
recycled wood or fiber
www.fsc.org Cert no. SW-COC-002358
© 1996 Forest Stewardship Council

FSC

97%

Printed and bound in Canada

To Ron & Margo,

for their wonderful hospitality 30 years ago,
when I came as an exchange student to the US:
this fantastic year allowed me to learn English
and radically changed my life!

I wish to express my deep gratitude: to my publisher,
Theodore Poulis, for his dedicated efforts to produce
an excellent translation of my book; to my translator,
Louis Marcelin-Rice, for his faithful rendering
of my thoughts; to my editor, Liadain Sherrard,
for her patient and very mindful revision of the final
draft; and to Dr Lewis Mehl-Madrona for the preface
he kindly wrote for this book. "Translation is reincarnation,"
said Hermann Graf von Keyserling, author of Travel Diary
of a Philosopher, *meaning that a faithful translation*
must free the original spirit of a text and give it a new
body. This is indeed what has been achieved here,
and I am grateful.

CONTENTS

Preface

Olivier Clerc's wonderful book builds upon a simple biological observation which he elevates to a profound observation about the human condition—that a frog will not
jump out of a pot of water when it is heated slowly. It remains in the water until it dies from the heat. Olivier's point,
I believe, is that we must work to maintain awareness. When
we fall for the quick-fix approach, we lose awareness and,
like the frog, may succumb to our own lack of sensitivity. He
says, "Like compliant frogs, many allow themselves to be
persuaded to remain passively in their broth which—for
sure!—will [not] turn into the nectar of health and the elixir of immortality." Furthermore, he says, "The great danger
of the principle of the frog in the pot of water is that as the
situation deteriorates, the faculties enabling the subject to
realize this deterioration are also impaired." This is the message of the book.

Olivier draws a wealth of meaning from the metaphor of
the Chinese bamboo, which knows how to work slowly and
in secret so that things may later grow swiftly and strongly
in the light. He writes about how the bamboo metaphor
teaches us not to trust in superficial appearances or messages which can be dangerously misleading. Humans, as it is

well known, are not well equipped to consider delayed effects in their causal reasoning process. This is particularly true in the world of allergies and immunology, where delayed hypersensitivity reactions (happening 36-72 hours after exposure to an antigen) are notoriously hard to appreciate, whereas direct, immediate allergic reactions, say to a bee sting, are easy to recognize.

Olivier also writes about the concept of critical mass in relation to social issues, similar to Malcolm Gladwell's concept of the "tipping point". He describes the spread of new ideas in these terms: that many people toil for years in relative obscurity until one day their idea catches on and, like wildfire spreading, becomes part of ordinary conversation, leading to a time when no one can imagine that people hadn't always embraced that new idea.

Invaluable Lessons from a Frog presents counter-narratives to those that suffuse contemporary, globalized, modernist, capitalism-based practices. The narratives that Olivier opposes are the "magic potion" story, "the quick-fix" story, the "linear cause-and-effect" story, and the "ignore the long-term consequences" story. These are just stories that we tell ourselves about how the world works. We tell them because others told them to us. We keep telling them because they run like a virus through the culture. Stories infect us, change us, and then we pass them on.

Another one of the metaphors Olivier uses is that of the butterfly. A butterfly must struggle free from its cocoon in order to develop and free its wings. Opening the cocoon for the butterfly will prevent it from flying at all. It must emerge on its own. Olivier likens successful healing to this same process. The healer removes obstacles that prevent the person's own emergence into health. The healer does not make them well, but, rather, reduces the blockages that prevent the person's own healing energy from taking care of the problem.

Over my career in medicine, and especially emergency medicine, I have come to agree with this observation. However impressive are our successes in trauma surgery and battlefield medicine, we do not perform so well with chronic disease. We try to "fix" it in the same way we fix a broken leg or sew a bleeding artery. Other medical systems, such as Ayurvedic or traditional Chinese or Native North American, attempt to remove the obstacles to the body's natural abilities for self-healing to work. In my work, I focus on helping people find stories to live that are more conducive to the health of their bodies than the ones that are contemporaneous with illness. To do this, we must first explore the source of those stories—who told them and in what contexts and why they are assumed to be the best or the only stories. Then, we need to replace them with other stories, the kind of stories of success over time that Olivier is promoting. We need caterpillar-to-butterfly stories to help us understand why the work of struggling out of the cocoon is so valuable.

Olivier presents spirituality as an antidote to groupthink, the dangerous homogenization of stories that serves the interests of globalized, modernist capitalism, because there are many different but equal spiritual paths. Contrary to religion, spirituality belongs to the person and can vary greatly among people, even within the same form of worship. Spirituality helps us to understand inner change that is transmitted to the outside, which represents a model of empowerment rather than being fixed from the outside.

Olivier finishes his "journey into the world of allegory" by commenting on the lessons we can learn from the metaphors that are natural phenomena. He says that nature is a great book: everything in it is symbolic and can speak to those who learn how to decipher its language. This journey, in his view, helps us to replace the narcissistic consciousness of modern humans, which is entirely self-centered and focused upon reflection, with a consciousness that is more intuitive, sensitive, and profound, that does not focus on appearances, that goes beyond the reflective surface of the mirror and arrives at a richer, more complete perception of the world. He argues that we transcend the fate of Narcissus, who became so hypnotized by his own reflection that he fell into the pond and died, by becoming more connected to each other, by reaching out to achieve an awareness of the interdependence of all beings and of their interconnectedness. As is taught by indigenous elders, we awaken through the deepening of our relationships —to each other, to nature, and to spirit—not, as is so popular, by looking within.

The power of Olivier's book lies in its timeliness as an alternative story or antidote to the quick-fix message which fills the airwaves and the bookshops and the cybernets of the world. People run from one quick fix to another, swiftly forgetting the former in their discovery of the next great world-saver. The danger here, as Olivier so well describes, is the deadening hypnotic effect of the perpetually new which inures us to any awareness of our slow disintegration. The metaphors of solution are elegant—the bamboo, giving illness time to heal, allowing systems and people to develop in their own ways and in accordance with their own proclivities—these are all helpful and useful. I strongly recommend this book as important reading for reinventing our lives in the 21st century and for awakening to our possibilities, many of which have been cleverly disguised by the factors described by Olivier.

Lewis Mehl-Madrona, M.D., Ph.D., M.Phil.
Clinical Assistant Professor,
University of Hawaii Department of Family Medicine
Associate Professor of Psychology, Argosy University, Hawaii
Author, *Coyote Medicine; Narrative Medicine; Narrative Psychiatry*

Introduction

All things are a language, everything speaks to us: natural phenomena, physical experiments, animal behavior, etc. Scientists have deduced laws based on their observation of the facts. For their part, poets, philosophers and wise men have found similarities and analogies between different phenomena and have expressed them in the symbolic and richly instructive language of metaphors or parables. These show up the underlying unity of phenomena that seem to be unrelated, but which in fact are governed by the same principles. As O.M. Aivanhov put it:

> The language of symbols, which is the only universal language, represents the quintessence of wisdom…Symbols are seeds you can plant; thus, you work with just a dozen symbols and you possess all knowledge…It is crucial to go deeper into this language of symbols, because by showing the links and correspondences between things, it reveals the profound unity of life.*

"*The profound unity of life*": this is the point. Metaphor and allegory affirm that the same forces, the same processes

---

* O.M. Aivanhov, *The Symbolic Language of Geometrical Figures*, Prosveta US.

and laws are at work on all levels, within us and around us, in the macrocosm and the microcosm, everywhere. The knowledge we derive from them is not analytic but synergic: it assembles, brings together, reveals connections.

Another advantage of metaphors, especially when they are derived from nature, is that they transcend centuries and millennia, as evidenced by the fact that the parables uttered by Jesus still speak to us today. The same is true of the symbols and images to be found in the Upanishads or in the Toltec tradition, for example. By contrast, have you ever tried to read a scientific text dating from the beginning of the 20th century (not to mention earlier centuries)?

Learning ages, knowledge does not. A sign is worn out in time, but not a symbol. A fruit perishes, a seed can survive for centuries. This is because symbols and images are given life by our own lives, our experience, our imagination. Hence the etymology of the French word for to know: connaître, "born with". Symbolic language is truly a bearer of knowledge: our participation is required for it to come alive.

Students of etymology will not fail to observe that the word "symbolic" is the opposite of the word "diabolic": sumbollein in Greek—literally "throw together"—means to assemble or bring together, whereas diabollein means to separate, to divide. The devil is, so to speak, the spirit of division, rather than a figure with horns, hooves, pointed tail and red skin. At a time when the analytical spirit rules supreme, encouraging rampant individualism and social fragmentation, and reducing the world to figures, statistics and lifeless data, symbols enable us to reintroduce life, poetry, imagination, connection and meaning into the world.

The seven metaphors and allegories I have chosen for this book all speak of awareness, of change, of evolution, and are inspired mostly by natural phenomena or physical experiments. Inevitably, their respective messages overlap, completing and enriching each other. In the unifying vision of symbolism, nothing is totally separate from anything else.

Obviously, each metaphor lends itself to several interpretations, to several readings which are not mutually exclusive, just as the symbol ☉, the circle and the dot, for example, can sometimes represent the sun, sometimes man and sometimes the whole universe. As you read this book, you will undoubtedly discover in the allegories of the narrative messages other than those proposed by me: so much the better. The purpose is precisely that these allegories should come alive in you and become your own, that they should become steeped in your being and imagination, so as to continue to nourish you, educate you and be useful to you, as they have been and still are to me.

All that remains is for me to wish you "*A good journey into the world of Allegory*"!

Olivier Clerc

The frog in a pot of water:
Are we already half cooked?

Imagine a pot filled with cold water with a frog quietly swimming in it. A fire is lit under the pot. The water slowly heats up. It is soon tepid. The frog finds this rather pleasant and continues swimming.

The temperature begins to rise. The water gets hot. It is a bit warmer than the frog would like, but he does not panic, especially as the warmth makes him tired and sleepy.

The water then gets really hot. The frog begins to find it unpleasant, but he is so weakened that he puts up with it, tries to adapt and does nothing.

The water temperature continues to rise gradually, without any abrupt change, until the frog is simply cooked and dies without ever getting out of the pot.

Thrown into a pot with water at 122° F, the same frog would immediately give a kick and flip healthily out of harm's way.[1]

This experiment[2] has a lot to teach us. It shows us that when deterioration takes place slowly enough, it slips past our awareness and mostly arouses no reaction in us, no opposition or rebellion. Isn't this just what we are seeing today in many areas of life?

---

1. It appears that this allegory was first written up in Marty Rubin's book, published in 1987, *The Boiled Frog Syndrome*.

2. ...which, obviously, I don't recommend.

Health, for instance, can deteriorate imperceptibly but surely. Illness is often the result of nourishment that is depleted, industrialized, tainted or even toxic, coupled with lack of exercise, stress and poorly managed emotions and relationships. Certain diseases establish themselves slowly, in 10, 20 or 30 years, the time it takes for our bodies and our psyches to reach saturation point with toxins, tensions, blockages, unexpressed thoughts and repressions. Our habituation to certain minor inconveniences, coupled with the loss of sensitivity and vitality, means that we fail to react to this imperceptible weakening of our health until illnesses that are more radical, more serious and harder to treat make their appearance.

Many couples, too, experience a progressive deterioration in their relationship. Who is able to say: "Our relationship started to go wrong on November 23 at 3 p.m."? The quality of relationships crumbles away little by little, for lack of maintenance. Unexpressed thoughts, misunderstandings and resentments accumulate without being dealt with, without our talking about them or trying together to find solutions. Like an untended garden, where weeds appear and where anarchy gradually takes over, a couple who do not maintain their relationship fail to see that it is deteriorating imperceptibly but steadily, until the situation becomes intolerable. Hence the high levels of divorce in modern society (not to mention the number of separations not recorded by the statistics).

With regard to agriculture and the environment, the allegory of the frog tells us about the gradual poisoning of the soil, air and water, far more insidious and dangerous than the obvious catastrophes reported in the media. Soils saturated with chemicals (in the form of fertilizers and pesticides), imperceptibly lose a bit more of their mineral content each year. As the years go by, more inputs are needed to make the land productive, so that soon we will be putting more into the earth than we will be getting out of it. Similarly, compared to the big episodes of pollution reported in the press, such as the oil spill from the *Prestige*, we have more to fear from the daily discharges from ships' tanks and the constant polluting of seas and oceans—these are far more dangerous due both to the scale on which they occur and to the fact that the effect is progressive, slow, barely visible, but devastating. This has meant that it has not, to date, produced any saving ecological "knee jerk" response which would rescue the frog—in other words us—from these foul waters.

On the level of society, we are witnessing a regular and constant decline of values, morals, and ethics. Year by year, this debasement of values takes place slowly, so that few of us are shocked by it. However, just like the frog plunged suddenly into water at a temperature of 122°, if one were to show an average American from the start of the 1980s a modern TV show or today's press coverage, his reaction would certainly be one of staggered incredulity. He would find it hard to believe that the time would come when articles would be written as mediocre in content and disrespectful in form as those we frequently read nowadays, or that such crass TV programs could be shown as those we are presented with on a daily basis. The increase in vulgarity and crudity, the disappearance of points of reference and of morality and the relativization of ethics have taken place in such a way—in slow motion—that very few people have noticed them or objected to them. In the same way, if we could be plunged into the year 2025 and see what the world has become by then, if it continues along the same course as now, we would probably be even more taken aback, given the fact that these developments seem to be taking place ever faster (an acceleration made possible because we are so bombarded by new information that we rapidly lose all stable terms of reference). Indeed, it should be noted that all futuristic films show the darkest of "super-technological" futures.

I could continue giving more examples of this phenomenon, for instance in politics or education, but the principle is in evidence all around us for anyone to see. Let me make it quite clear, however, that by highlighting this slow process of decline, I am not doom-mongering, nor am I idealizing some bygone era when health, family values and morality were perfect. Such a past is clearly mythical. In making these observations, my intention is rather to point out that when a situation results from a process which takes place over a *long period*, any rapid and short-term solutions are generally inadequate, if they do not actually aggravate the situation in the long run. It is therefore not a question of going backwards, to a so-called ideal past, but of discerning, in our attempts to improve the present, what are merely fleeting illusions and superficial props and patches.

Thus, with regard to health, our refusal to take into account this slow deterioration leads us to consume more and more drugs and to undergo an increasing number of treatments of all kinds. The colossal "health care" costs (which are in fact illness costs), far from being a sign of a progressively healthier society, actually indicate a health policy which ignores the deep and lasting causes of illness and which, by providing only rapid, symptom-oriented and superficial solutions, contributes in the long term to longer-lasting and ever more complex diseases. Only a *long-term* policy of prevention and health education would allow a re-orientation of this drift into hyper-medication, given that it would take at least one generation before we would begin to see any results.

Similarly, in the case of society, we will not stop the development of violence and delinquency, closely linked to the above-mentioned loss of values, simply by multiplying the means of repression, the number of policemen, security agents and closed-circuit TV cameras. If we do not take into account the deeper global causes of this phenomenon, going back several decades, any quick-fix solutions we resort to—which for election purposes must obviously be rapid and supposedly effective (or at least appear to be so)—will only provide us with a brief reprieve before the problem recurs on a larger scale. Modern Western society thus resembles a punctured ball that is deflating and that we are clumsily trying to knock back into shape by putting glue on it: since we are unable to breathe more soul into a society that desperately lacks it, we try to firm up its structure by means of laws and decrees of all sorts, the increasing number of which is a clear sign of bad moral health.

What the allegory of the frog teaches us, then, is that whenever a process of deterioration is slow, slight and almost imperceptible, we need either a very acute consciousness or a good memory to realize that it is happening, or else a reliable yardstick whereby we can assess the situation. It seems, however, that all three of these things are now rare.

1) Without *consciousness*, we become less than human, moved only by instincts and automatic reactions. Consciousness is therefore an essential condition of our humanity: no real thought, no reflection and no free will are possible in the absence of consciousness. Lacking consciousness, man is asleep, whether actually or figuratively. This is why "awakening" is at the heart of all forms of spirituality.[3]

2) Deprived of *memory*, we could spend each waking day in the darkness of night (and vice versa) without in the least realizing it, because changes in light intensity are too

---

3. Some even go as far as teaching how to become conscious in dreams, such as the Toltec way, as described by Carlos Castaneda, or in Tibetan Buddhism, especially in the Six Yogas of Naropa, one of which is devoted to the dream state.

slow and weak to be perceived by the human eye.[4] It is memory that makes us aware *a posteriori* of the alternation of day and night, as it is memory that enables us to measure all the subtle developments that take place in and around us, at a very slow rate. Without memory there would be no comparison, no discernment, and therefore no development.

3) Lastly, one of the reasons the frog ends up being cooked, so to speak, is that it has no thermometer other than its skin to gauge the gradual increase of temperature: it has no viable *yardstick* by which to evaluate the situation as it develops. And when it comes to us, what are our standards? How do we evaluate the "ambient temperature"? With reference to what do we determine the quality of our life, of our health, and of society?

Before we weigh ourselves, we check that the scales are set on zero. Before we use a measuring instrument, we calibrate it, otherwise its measurements are not reliable. But what of our own inner "instruments"? Do we know what the social, cultural, family, religious and other influences are that have calibrated them, often unbeknown to us?

What allows things to deteriorate without provoking any reaction on our part is probably our excessive confidence in our own personal judgments—which are necessarily subjective—in conjunction with our readiness to doubt the older collective standards, which have been replaced by others that are variable. The older standards were established by religions, which showed, on the one hand, abysses

---

4. Incidentally, I discovered the premises of this allegory of the frog at high school, when I was put in charge of the lighting of a stage production: the director had asked me to make all the changes in the intensity of the lighting so slowly that the audience would be unable to notice them. I was amazed to see that indeed, below a certain level of speed, only memory could indicate, by comparison, that the situation had changed.

hedged around by prohibitions and, on the other, ideals to which to aspire. A parallel may be drawn with the manner in which a thermometer is created, by noting on a tube filled with mercury the level that is reached when it is dipped in boiling water and then in freezing water, and graduating the space that separates the two levels. Although the choice of the system of gradation is arbitrary, water always boils and freezes under the same conditions, whether it is measured in Celsius or Fahrenheit. Similarly, whichever religion we take as our reference point, the most laudable and the most criminal acts remain the same, even if each tradition has its own nuances. The new moral and spiritual standards, however, no longer furnish us with any higher perspective, but merely point us to a lower level where, today, we are expected to set the bar a little lower still. Idealism has become outdated. "How low can we go?" seems to be the modern motto. Today's immorality thus becomes tomorrow's morality, in a Dantesque plunge towards the lowest degrees of *humanness*.

In saying this, I am not advocating religious fundamentalism nor affiliation to established religion—although I do not reject the latter—but rather the necessity of equipping ourselves with a system of references which possesses a non-negotiable lower limit and above all an ideal to aim for. Without a vision of an attainable height, how can we progress? Without a horizon to aim for, why bother to move? An ideal is a remedy both for the status quo and for a decline.

Results:

- Stupefied by too much sensory stimulation,
  our consciousness goes to sleep.
- Crammed with useless information,
  our memory is blunted.
- Deprived of standards, we no longer have
  any fixed points of reference.

• Suffocated by materialism and consumerism,
our idealism shrivels and dies.

The frog, unaware, amnesiac and bored, has only to let it-self be cooked. And this is how part of society sinks into moral and spiritual obscurity, with social disintegration, environ-mental degradation, the Faustian drift of genetics and bio-technology, and the stupefying of the masses—among other symptoms—through which this process becomes global.

The principle of the frog in a pot of water is a trap we should never underestimate if our ideal is the quest for quality, for development, for perfection, if we refuse medi-ocrity, the status quo and inaction. Indeed, matter left to it-self is governed by the law of entropy. If we do not take care of something but abandon it, it wastes away, declines, degrades, be it a body, a relationship, a garden, the social organization of a country, etc. Everything requires mainte-nance, energy, vigilance and effort.

Effort?

This word is starting to be viewed as indecent. "Lose weight without any effort", "Get rich without any effort", "Open all your chakras and reach illumination without any effort": these slogans (or other no less explicit variants) are bandied around by many of the mass media. "Everything, right now, without any effort…and if possible for free": this is the ideal they are currently trying to sell us. "Let us do it, we will take care of everything!" we are told. Oh really? To cap it all, some authors do not hesitate to pervert several spiritual principles in order to justify a so-called "illuminat-ed" form of inaction, which is supposed to bring success at every level to its followers: prosperity is close at hand, the universe is "conspiring" to make us rich and happy…Like compliant frogs, many allow themselves to be persuaded to remain passively in their broth which—for sure!—will turn into the nectar of health and the elixir of immortality.

All this is obviously utter nonsense. Without effort, without a constant input of energy, things simply fade out. And the instant facility that we are offered—free of charge!—generally hides a steep bill to be paid later, as the story of Dr Faustus illustrates.

The great danger of the principle of the frog in the pot of water is that as the situation deteriorates, *the faculties enabling the subject to realize this deterioration are also impaired.* It is like a tired driver falling asleep at the wheel, because the greater his fatigue, the less conscious he is of subsiding and the less he perceives that he is dropping off, that his eyes, instead of just blinking, are staying closed longer and longer. The French singer Georges Brassens used to sing:

> *Entre nous soit dit, braves gens,*
> *Pour reconnaître,*
> *Que l'on est pas intelligent,*
> *Il faudrait l'être.*
> [Between you and me, dear people,
> To acknowledge
> That we are not intelligent,
> We would need to be so.]

Similarly, to realize that I am unconscious, I would need to be conscious. To realize that I have lost my alertness, I would need to be alert. The paradox of personal development is that at every stage, I become aware retrospectively of the degree to which, in the preceding stage, I was not free, conscious, or enlightened, in relation to the level I have now reached. Knowing this, it would be wise on our part to recognize the relative and limited character of our present awareness and its perceptions and realizations, and not to attach more credit to them than they deserve. We should strive constantly to surpass ourselves, to attain a higher awareness and a truer perception. In other words, we should cultivate a healthy form of doubt: not the kind that prevents progress, that undermines and criticizes everything, but the kind that is not satisfied with appearances, the kind that moves us to verify, to go further, to question things, to question ourselves and our convictions.

In a more general sense, *how do we avoid falling into the trap of the frog in the pot of water, individually or collectively?*

On the one hand, by never ceasing to broaden and increase our awareness, and on the other by honing our memory so as to retain points of comparison between the past and the present. Also, we avoid the trap by referring to reliable standards in order to assess any changes—standards we must carefully select as being the least subject to the fluctuations of fashion, period and any sort of trend. In short, by making ideals the fuel of our continual impulse to go beyond ourselves.

It is no coincidence that the training and development of consciousness is something common to all spiritual practices: awareness of self, awareness of the body, consciousness of language, awareness of thoughts and emotions, awareness of others, higher states of consciousness. Beyond all dogmas, doctrines, and ideologies, we should regard the broadening and deepening of our consciousness—rather than the development of our merely intellectual faculties—as fundamental to our status as human beings, and as the driving force behind our evolution.

As regards memory, in an over-informed world it is vital for us to know how to prioritize our memories, by affixing the seal of consciousness to the most important ones, and by practicing selective forgetfulness[5] so as to make room for

---

5. Various works suggest that nothing is completely forgotten, that everything leaves a trace. By "selective forgetfulness" I mean above all the freeing up of one's "live memory", the one we use most often, as opposed to our "dead memory", the "hard disk" which contains all our memories, buried more or less deeply.

what is essential. In French, there are two ways of talking about memorizing: we can know something "in our head", or we can learn it "by heart". What we know "in our head" is soon forgotten: it's the lesson we learn for the exam, that we forget the next day. What we have learned "by heart", however, stays with us for years: the memory is not just airy and in the mind, like a balloon rising up through the air as soon as we let go of it: it is much denser, it has sunk into us, like a sponge soaked in liquid; its ink leaves a trace deep within us. If we wish to remember important things, we must be passionate about them, take them to heart, both literally and figuratively.

Finally, as far as standards and ideals are concerned, references and sources of inspiration are widely available. Of course, one may no longer feel attuned to the tradition one was raised in, or may consider that certain precepts no longer fit the present time; but although the form may change and evolve, the spirit remains. Let us not throw the baby out with the bathwater. We are lucky to live at a time when the wisdom of the civilizations of the whole world and of all time is available to most of us; a time, moreover, when representatives of various traditions have labored to rephrase their messages in a way that makes them relevant to our era and accessible to all.[6] There are more references and inspirations to be found there than we'll ever need.

One last word before finishing with this first allegory. The general principle of the metaphor—the fact that we do not perceive progressive change, and the consequent lack of reaction to it—can also work in a positive manner, even though it would be better to find another allegory for it that doesn't end up with a boiled frog. Indeed, the changes

---

6. Examples include O.M. Aivanhov for the Christian message, Lama Yeshe for the Tibetans, Don Miguel Ruiz for the Toltecs, Sobonfu Somé for African wisdom, and many others.

occurring within us and around us, on a small or large scale, are not purely negative: far from it. Even when they are positive, they may go unnoticed. On an individual level, for instance, the efforts a person makes on a daily basis to become better (inner work, meditation, prayer) do not yield any obvious short-term results. Similarly, the evolution of civil rights or of working conditions, for example, has also happened slowly, over many decades. When we fail to notice these changes—positive changes, this time—we likewise suffer unfortunate consequences, even though these differ from the consequences of failing to notice negative changes. If we do not see the results of our inner work, we may get discouraged and give up, whereas with a little more perseverance we would all at once see our efforts rewarded. Similarly, if we do not perceive the advantages we enjoy and the rights we benefit from, we may nourish ungratefulness and discontent, and be unable to appreciate the fruits of an evolution that is undeniably slow, but sure.

Consequently, the most important aspect of this allegory of the frog is *unawareness of change*, whether this change is negative or positive, since in either case the lack of awareness is harmful to us. The primary remedy is the same in both cases: consciousness, consciousness and more consciousness. Everything else depends on it: what's the use of memory, of standards and ideals, if we are unconscious?

In relation to this, here is a little anecdote, taken from my first book (now out of print), written when I was 20 years old.[7] I was trying to become conscious in my dreams, so as to reproduce the experiences I had read about in various books on spirituality. Given the poor results I had with the methods I found in the books, I decided to develop my own. Logically, I thought that to become conscious

---

7. O. Clerc, *Vivre ses rêves: techniques pour programmer ses rêves et induire des rêves lucides*, Hélios, 1983.

in my dreams, I had to be more conscious in my waking life. So, I wrote a big "C" on my left hand with a felt-tip pen, to remind myself as many times as possible during the day to be conscious. Each time I saw that "C" (which was very often), I would make a "consciousness pause" of a few seconds: I would stop whatever I was doing, and become conscious of where I was, who I was, what choices were available to me, of my free will, etc. Less than a week after having started this practice, I started making "consciousness pauses" in the middle of my dreams, which allowed me to have frequent lucid dreams, which I could control as I wanted. But, in the end, these lucid dreams were secondary to the benefit of having heightened my daily consciousness in all the situations of my life. In dreams, when you become conscious, all your perceptions are suddenly heightened: light is stronger, colors more vivid, sound (one's own voice, in particular) is louder. In the waking state, an increased awareness similarly intensifies the quality of our life.

From Plato's Allegory of the Cave to the recent movie *The Matrix*, and in the mass of spiritual writings in between, the need to be conscious, "to awaken", not to trust our dream perceptions, has always been repeatedly stressed. At a time when some people are trying to turn *Homo sapiens* into *Homo zappiens*, with mindless overdoses of TV (the modern version of Plato's cave, where color images replace the shadows projected on the walls), we should be promoting *Homo consciens*, the conscious and awakened man, escaped at last out of the bubbling soup of today's culture. It's the only way to frog-march him out of his present predicament!

The Chinese bamboo:
Preparation in the dark

It is said that there is a very special variety of bamboo in China. If you sow a seed of this type in fertile ground, you have to be very patient. Indeed, the first year nothing happens: no stem deigns to come out of the earth, not even the tiniest shoot. Neither does it in the second year. The third, then? Nothing at all. What about the fourth? Alas, no. It is only in the fifth year that this bamboo finally sticks the tip of its stem out of the soil. But then, it will grow 40 feet high in just one year: a spectacular "catch-up"! The reason is simple: for five years, whereas nothing happens on the surface, the bamboo is secretly developing prodigious roots in the ground, and those roots, when the time has come, allow it to make a triumphant entry into the visible world, in full daylight.

The metaphor of the frog refers to changes that happen very slowly and imperceptibly. The metaphor of the Chinese bamboo speaks of a sudden, rapid, and spectacular change. However, as we shall see, both are closely linked.

The Chinese bamboo allegory incorporates a number of very important teachings. First of all, it shows us that just because we don't see anything it doesn't mean that nothing is happening. Second, it shows that some sudden or instantaneous changes may be the result of a slow evolution which is itself imperceptible.

This is what happens, for instance, in chemistry when making a precipitate: you hold two tubes, each filled with a different transparent liquid; you pour the contents of one tube into the other, drop by drop, very slowly. No difference is seen, until the moment when you add one more drop from the first tube to the second—just one—and off you go!—it triggers a precipitate, the whole solution becomes blue and crystallizes suddenly. If you hadn't seen all the preceding drops and you saw only the last drop being added, you might hastily conclude that it was that one last drop alone that triggered the whole reaction.

A similar phenomenon is found in electricity with condensers. These devices (used for instance for the indicators or the windshield wipers in our cars) accumulate electricity until a certain charge is reached, at which point all the electrical current is suddenly released, activating a lamp or a motor.

One last example taken from physics involves the electrons of an atom that gravitate around the nucleus, in different orbits, each of which corresponds to a precise level of energy. No electron may gravitate *between* these orbits. This means that to change orbit, an electron must accumulate *all* the energy which separates its own orbit from the next. If that electron has 90% of the energy of the next orbit, it stays in its present orbit. We do not see the energy that it has accumulated until it suddenly moves to a new orbit, the moment it reaches the energy threshold necessary to cross the gap. This amount of energy is called a *quantum*: therefore, we speak of a *quantum leap* when an electron changes orbit. By extension, this term is now used to describe any radical change which can only happen when a certain preliminary level of energy has been reached. Likewise, the Chinese bamboo will only make its extraordinary 40-foot growth after having developed a sufficient network of roots to provide it with all the sap necessary for such a feat.

At the human level, the Chinese bamboo phenomenon can be observed in many different areas. If we are unaware of it, we may often misinterpret various situations, by being unnecessarily alarmed by an apparent lack of positive changes. Alternatively, our calm and assurance may be based on a deceptive absence of negative changes, which will, however, make an appearance soon.

In the field of education, for instance, some children progress in a consistent and regular manner, whereas others seem to stagnate and to fall further and further behind. Yet among the latter we often find "bamboo kids" who, having reached a certain stage of their imperceptible inner maturation, will suddenly make giant strides in their development, catching up with and often overtaking the other students, compared to whom they had seemed behind. By way of example, it is said that Einstein only started talking when he was three, and that at age seven, he was considered "retarded". A better knowledge of the psychology of each child—there are plenty of tests for that[8]—would enable us to sort out these kids from the ones who are really retarded. Parents and educators would thus avoid worrying pointlessly, and these kids with a *quantum* development would no longer be under so much pressure. Pressure will not speed up their natural evolution, any more than a seed will grow more quickly if you threaten it.

The Chinese bamboo is also found in the fields of personal development, psychotherapy and even spirituality. In contrast to the intellectual knowledge that we tend to acquire in a linear manner, by accumulating and memorizing various facts, the changes that affect our psyche—our heart, feelings, emotions, the marks of our past—and the changes

---

8. What is mostly lacking is time and availability to identify these cases, since in public education classes are often too large for teachers to have a personal relationship with each student.

that affect our subtle dimension—our soul and spirit—happen most of the time in a bamboo manner. Thus, for instance, mere intellectual understanding of the psychological issues linked with our childhood is rarely sufficient to trigger any change or emotional release in us. It is only when the *emotional charge* of our life experience (we come back to the idea of a charge, mentioned above) finds expression that we suddenly reach a new level of consciousness. Some psychotherapists even stimulate this process by asking their patients to adopt a diet of raw fruits and vegetables, so as to increase the number of electrolytes in their bodies, which contributes to this emotional release.[9] Likewise, on the spiritual level, most meditation methods, disciplines and practices do not yield immediate results (the bad news is that to begin with they can appear to make the practitioners worse![10]). It is only after months or—more often—years of practice that a transformation takes place, sometimes in a very short time.[11] The followers of any spiritual discipline who are unaware of this slow, unseen transformation, the prelude to attaining a new state of consciousness or the awakening of new faculties, may lose courage. They may even decide that all their efforts are useless and unproductive, even though they might be just a few steps away from success. Beyond the principle itself of the Chinese bamboo, we should know that nothing is ever lost, that all efforts yield results sooner or later, even though most of the time no one can know when exactly these results will come about.

---

9. On this subject, see *Deep Feeling, Deep Healing* by Andy Bernay-Roman, Spectrum Healing Press, 2001.

10. This worsening is often only in appearance and is the result of the extra awareness acquired through these practices.

11. On this question, see especially *Le soufisme, au cœur de l'Islam*, by Cheikh Khaled Bentounès, in which he tells of the rapid transformation that took place in him on the death of his father, when he was appointed as his spiritual successor.

On the negative side, the metaphor of the Chinese bamboo may also have some unpleasant surprises in store, in a manner both similar to and different from the metaphor of the frog. In the frog metaphor, change is slow, but it remains perceptible for anyone with an acute awareness or a good memory. But in the case of the Chinese bamboo, change is not perceptible but hidden, underground; it can only be perceived by using specific methods, by digging under the earth, so as to see what is happening at a subtle level, before it materializes.

As regards health, certain types of behavior (such as smoking, for instance) or certain deficiencies (such as lack of iron) trigger a slow deterioration which can nevertheless be observed, if we are alert enough. Therefore, they correspond to the story of the frog. Other changes, however, belonging to the bamboo category, are imperceptible to our ordinary senses. They only become brutally obvious when it is late, if not *too* late. An unbalanced diet, for instance, will make your bones fragile or will cause your circulatory system to deteriorate, slowly paving the way for various fractures or cardiovascular episodes. Both fractures and heart attacks are the last and most brutal evidence of a deterioration to which we have paid no attention.

Similarly, in agriculture, the use of chemical fertilizers and pesticides creates an imperceptible but dangerous dearth of minerals in the soil that is invisible to the naked eye[12] and that—once it has passed the tipping-point—triggers an irreversible process of desertification. Entire regions could one day suddenly turn into deserts, as has already happened —for other reasons—to those once green and fertile lands, Iraq and Iran.

---

12. Unless a scientific analysis is carried out on the soils or the fruit and vegetables they produce.

In other words, the greatest dangers are often not the most visible. When there is an oil slick on the sea, everybody can see it. But when the fragile balance of the composition of seawater, which is indispensable to the plants and fish which depend on it, is disturbed, when some of its components go missing or are present in excess, we do not see it. It is sometimes the sudden disappearance of a vegetable or animal species that alerts us to a decline that has gone unnoticed, because certain basic nutrients, essential for their survival, are no longer available to them.

The bamboo allegory thus teaches us not to trust in appearances that may be dangerously misleading. From the greenhouse gases, some of which take 30 years to reach a level of the atmosphere where they will cause damage, to the daily exposure to high voltage lines which, after several years, end up causing cancers, we can see that all the phenomena related to this allegory possess a "delayed action" factor which, if not taken into account, can have fatal consequences.

We also find in the Chinese bamboo metaphor the concept of "critical mass", often mentioned today, for example, in relation to social issues. When there is an attempt to promote a new idea, there can be a relatively long period during which all efforts to do so seem to have no effect, or very little. Then one day—no one knows when—a corner is turned and suddenly the idea starts spreading like a powder trail and everyone is talking about it. Soon, there comes a point where we can no longer even imagine a time when this idea was unknown. Take pedophilia, for instance. It is not a new phenomenon, nor something that has suddenly increased. What has actually happened is that the untiring efforts of a few organizations to heighten public awareness about the issue have suddenly reached a "critical mass", that is, a large enough number of informed people, and all at once, like the bamboo stem, the issue comes to light and we all become aware of it.

In a different context, Elisabeth Kübler-Ross, pioneer of support for terminally ill patients, has described how she tried all alone to increase the awareness of the medical profession on this issue. She worked and fought tirelessly to promote the idea that dying people need to be supported, up to the point where, having encountered nothing but hostility and denigration, she was so exhausted and desperate that she decided to give up. It was then, she said, that the most unbelievable event of her life took place. The day she decided to tell her boss that she was resigning, one of the people she had supported up to their death appeared in her office (!) to tell her not to give up, because her work would soon bear results. Without this intervention from the other world, Elisabeth Kübler-Ross would never have known that she was just a step away from reaching her goal. She would not have seen that all of her efforts, far from being fruitless, had woven a powerful network of underground roots, out of which a promising stem was soon to spring up into the light. Indeed, just a few months after this disturbing event, her work started to arouse an interest which has been increasing ever since, to the point that today, offering support to terminally ill people seems obvious, something that has always existed.

In our times, when the cult of immediacy has taken on extreme proportions—"Everything, right now, without any effort", as I said above—the metaphor of the Chinese bamboo teaches us perseverance, long-term work, and the refusal to resign ourselves. *"You need a few weeks to grow a salad, but a hundred years to make an oak,"* O.M. Aivanhov would often say, to point out that great things are never done in a day. As compared to an oak, the Chinese bamboo presents the additional difficulty of hiding its ongoing underground development, which doesn't allow us to measure its progress. So we must persevere, in the absence of any tangible evidence that what we are doing is of use. In other words, the Chinese bamboo teaches us to work with *time*, Chronos, old Saturn; to sow today and harvest later: in a day, a week, a year, or more. Whereas children live in the present moment—having to wait five minutes seems like an eternity to them; they want immediate and rapid results—we discover with age, and the wisdom that is supposed to come with it, how to work in the long term and how to make time our ally, no longer our enemy. Furthermore, we should note that over and above opinions and fashions, and the fluctuating judgments of each generation, time remains the surest and most ruthless judge of human endeavors: only quality, in the form of beauty, goodness, truth and justice, can withstand its wear and tear. Everything else succumbs.

Conversely, when we want to go too fast, when we do not take the time to develop deep roots before reaching for the sky, we run the risk of producing something weak and fragile, with not enough sap to nourish its branches and bear fruit. This is as true for plants as for human beings and the works they create.

At a time like this, when so many people talk about insecurity, when the means of repression keep increasing, when we lament the rise of various forms of violence and criminality, we should reflect, well before all these problems occur, on the conditions under which our children *take root* in the soil of life during the first months of their existence. With only a few weeks of maternity leave, it is hard for a baby with a working mother to develop a network of deep and stabilizing roots in the maternal soil. This requires at least a year, ideally two or three. But instead, no sooner has the little human sprout started to develop its connection with the mother than it is uprooted, doomed to soilless culture, going from nannies to day-care centers and a succession of baby-sitters. This is where we must chiefly look to find the deep roots of insecurity and the resulting antisocial behaviors, as the psychotherapists can report who are daily confronted with young adults raised in these conditions. But, as with the Chinese bamboo, the time spent in taking care of and educating infants doesn't bear immediate fruits: it is only 10, 15 or 20 years later that you see the difference between those who were able to develop a good root-system and those who weren't. Because of this time lapse, some people question the correlation between the quality of the first years of life and what happens later on. Yet there is enough evidence today to convince us of how significant this rooting process is for the development of "human bamboos"![13]

On the other hand, when we are familiar with the principle of the Chinese bamboo and we elect to work with it, it becomes very interesting indeed. Before birth, a baby spends nine months in the dark of its mother's womb. Before it germinates, a seed spends some time under the ground, in the dark. And in the book of Genesis, each day starts with the night: *"And the evening and the morning were the nth day"* we read for each day of the Creation. In a similar manner, most of our undertakings and projects need to mature for a certain time in darkness before we can bring them out into the light of day. If we do it too early, they are nipped in the bud. Light nourishes and animates whatever lives under the sun, but it can destroy and kill embryonic life forms that need to grow larger and stronger, hidden in the earth, the womb or in our imagination. In traditional photography, the film needs

---

13. Read especially *The Continuum Concept* by Jean Liedloff, Duckworth, 1975.

to be removed from the camera and undergo several chemical baths before being exposed to the light, in case the negatives end up as white blanks. Similarly, our projects must have a "thorough soaking", must be permeated and nourished by our feelings, strong and solid, before we talk about them to others and bring them out into the light. Words, if used improperly, can drain the sap out of an idea or a project, and deprive it of roots.

Drawing strength from its powerful roots, the extraordinary growth of the Chinese bamboo puts it rapidly out of the reach of predators. On the other hand, young plants which put out their brave but delicate shoots too early may soon become a tidbit for some herbivore or fall prey to insects and parasites. Therefore, the bamboo metaphor teaches us the value of a silent preparation and of secrecy: not the shameful secret that we must hide at all costs, nor the unhealthy secret of some criminal enterprise, but the secret of creation, the secret of the "black phase" of alchemy, without which there can be no gold, the secret of the primordial void out of which all creation arose.

It is not a coincidence that the reproductive organs of women are hidden, whereas those of men are fully visible: secrecy is feminine in essence, it is the womb of worlds, the nourishing earth, the fertile darkness out of which light springs forth, it is the Word that precedes speech. Just as a woman keeps her baby in her womb for many months before presenting it to the world, so too the artist and creator must carry their project in their heart and spirit, nourishing it over a long period with their love, their inspiration and their hope, before revealing it to the eyes of others. Ideas and projects are seeds nourished by the sap of our heart, in order to be given life by our hands and take root in reality. Left on the ground, instead of being wisely buried under the soil, seeds fly away, blown by the

wind, and no one knows in what unknown soil they may finally come to life.

The Chinese bamboo yields a wealth of allegorical meaning. To know how to work slowly and in secret, so that
things may later grow swiftly and strongly in the light. To
learn to perceive some silent, underground development,
whether this be positive or negative, behind a calm appearance. To make a conscious ally of time, instead of an unconscious enemy. With the bamboo, we set foot in the invisible,
the subtle world. We escape a little from the jail of manifes-
tation in order to explore the source of the possible. From
the visible effects we go back to the hidden causes.

Like the bamboo, like all plants, man acts as a link: from
his observation of concrete facts, he derives conclusions
and laws; he extracts the subtle from the dense, as a tree
manufactures its sweet fruits out of the raw sap of its roots;
and out of ideas and inspiration, man gives a concrete form
to his projects, life to his dreams, and body to his creations,
just as the fruit falls from the tree so that its seeds can give
birth to new trees. By applying to ourselves the symbolic
language of nature, we see, time and again, that the same
principles are operative everywhere.

Wax and hot water:[14]
The power of first impressions

Imagine a bowl containing a thick layer of cold, hardened wax, with a completely flat and smooth surface. You take a jug full of hot water and pour a little onto the wax. The water can spread freely over the surface, unobstructed by any contours. But, being hot, as soon as it comes into contact with the wax, the water melts the wax, leaving a shallow impression like that of a skier in powder snow. The wax now contains a slight hollow where the hot water has made a channel like the bed of a river. If you then pour a little more hot water into the bowl, what happens? Regardless of where it falls, the water is now less free to spread than it was the first time round, and it will inevitably run into the existing track which will guide its flow and will itself become a little deeper. The more hot water you pour on, the deeper the channel that is created, leaving the water no choice but to follow the path already carved out.

What does this metaphor tell us? That a first imprint, a first impression (in all senses of the word) leaves a *trace*, and that this strongly influences subsequent imprints. Isn't this how brooks, streams, rivers and even canyons are formed?

---

14. This metaphor is drawn from the works of Edward de Bono: *Lateral Thinking, Serious Creativity, Five-Day Course in Thinking* and *Why So Stupid?*

The contours of the earth's surface have not always been as we know them today. The water of the first rains that poured down on certain regions, millions of years ago, flowed along existing contours—mountains, valleys and rocks—and its passage or accumulation in certain places traced the first outlines of future water courses and lakes, which the passage of time further defined and deepened.

Can we change these tracks once they are made? Yes, since we have acquired the capacity to modify—often misguidedly—the course of brooks, streams and even huge rivers. But the deeper the track, the more powerful the flow along it, and the more substantial are the means required to change its course. This is a first observation. Moreover, diverting a watercourse from its bed is one thing; erasing the traces of its previous flow is another. Even if the water now follows the new course which has been forced on it, the original bed can continue to exist for a very long time, even when it has dried out, with the risk that at some unforeseen moment, flash floods may once again pour through the conveniently available channel.

On the human level, this principle of the wax and hot water can be seen to operate in many forms. For instance, look at the way a first impression of a person leaves a snapshot within us that influences all subsequent encounters and which is very difficult to eradicate if this impression happens to be mistaken. It is said that *you get only one chance to make a good first impression*: this may be a truism, but it expressly draws attention to the frequently underestimated impact of any *first appearance*. A bad impression, whatever one says, is never completely erased: even if we go on to develop an excellent relationship with somebody in spite of this false start, years later an incident or a misunderstanding can suddenly revive the first impression and even lead us to cast doubt on the positive aspects of the

years in between. Needless to say, I am not promoting fa-
talism but awareness—a constant theme of this book. Indeed, knowledge of this principle can make us more vigi-
lant and increase our awareness of each beginning, each
first appearance and each unfolding of a new situation.

For example, an experienced musician must know that
the first reading of a musical score is crucial and should therefore be undertaken slowly, being sure to make no mistakes.
If he gets it right the first time, the chances are he will get
it right on subsequent occasions. On the other hand, a wrong
note or an awkward fingering at this stage will tend to slip
automatically into the musician's future playing as soon as
his concentration lapses. Indeed, the musician's hands are
the wax in which the flow of the melody leaves its impression, so that later on kinesthetic memory (the memory of
the body) will guide the fingers to the same notes as the
first time. Once the score has been wrongly read, it takes
dozens, if not hundreds, of rehearsals to correct the original impression, monopolizing the musician's awareness,
which should be concentrated on the interpretation and
not focused on the fingering.

In a more general sense, one can see the importance of
this analogy of wax and hot water for everything that re-
lates to education and learning, whether in sport, DIY, martial arts, dance, driving or the way in which a child learns
to read, write, tie shoelaces or perform the thousands of
gestures involved in everyday life,[15] or even in the use of computer programs. The energy we spend on *correcting* something
that has been wrongly learned at the start is many times

---

15. Montessori schools, for instance, spend a great deal of time teach-
     ing very small children to handle fragile objects—glasses, carafes,
     glass or porcelain cups—and to perform daily gestures with pre-
     cision, so that they are much less clumsy than children who have
     not been taught in this way.

greater than the energy we would have expended in exercising the extra attention and awareness required to get it right from the very beginning.[16] By trying to go too fast initially, we substantially slow down the attainment of the desired result. "Drive slowly, I'm in a hurry," Churchill wisely told his chauffeur.

With the metaphor of the wax and the hot water we discover the importance of every *beginning*. When we say that someone has "got up on the wrong side of the bed" we mean that this person has started the day badly and that as a result all the rest of the day has been affected. In fact, we find that many religions issue injunctions about how to start the day: with a prayer, a positive thought, a blessing, a constructive act of any sort. We cannot be aware of everything all the time: inevitably we are swamped by tasks, at work or at home, for longer or shorter periods. This is why by starting out to do something consciously and positively, we trace the route and set the course which will then be followed when we activate the "automatic pilot".

A life or even a day contains many "beginnings". From the "Good morning!" we exchange with our family or colleagues, to a marriage, the creation of a business, moving into a new house, the first meeting of a new partnership, the first documents (logos, texts) that embody the image of a new business, the advertisements we send out, etc. We have a vested interest in identifying these beginnings and in devoting special attention to them: it is a wise policy that avoids many subsequent problems. This is obviously not a panacea, nor is it a guarantee that no problems will arise at

---

16. "Right", not perfectly: perfection comes with practice and training. A score can be read right the first time, but it will have to be played hundreds of times before a successful interpretation is achieved—"practice makes perfect".

some point in the future. But in this way we give ourselves more of a chance *from the start*.

Insofar as it denotes a beginning, an initial, *first* imprint, this story of the wax and hot water deals implicitly with the other extreme: *the end*. Logically, if there is a beginning, it means that something before it has come to an end. Thus the end and the beginning are linked. What is the first thought that comes to us in the morning? Nine times out of ten it is the one we went to sleep with. It is not for nothing that students are advised to revise lessons just before going to sleep: the unconscious ensures that our last thoughts are deeply engraved in our memory, and as a logical consequence, this imprint sets the course of the first thoughts that arise in us the following morning.

From Christ's injunction to make peace with one's brother *before the sun goes down* to the recommendations of many religions to die in peace having first forgiven others, along with the *happy ending* of most films, the polite formulas at the end of even the most unpleasant letters, or the advice often given to end a meditation session before fatigue and pain appear, there are plenty of examples that illustrate the importance of a good ending, even when things have gotten off to a bad start. For the end, too, leaves a trace, an imprint. For instance, I remember two films—*Le prix du danger*, with Gérard Lanvin, and Terry Gilliam's *Brazil*—whose very sinister endings haunted me for days. If a sad film has a happy ending, what we will remember best is the last scene which rapidly erases the somber episodes that preceded it. On the other hand, in the case of a pleasant film that ends tragically the conclusion will stick in our throat for a long time. Imagine if a magnificent concert ended with a discord: what kind of impression would we come away with?

A good beginning, therefore, paves the way for a good ending. A good start enhances a good run and makes a good end more likely, and so on. The two moments when we have the most influence on events are thus the beginning and the end. These are the moments when our conscious choices have the greatest chance of modifying the course of things. Incidentally, publishers and authors are well aware of this: the former take great care over the choice of a book's cover and title page, and of its end page; the latter pay special attention to the introduction to their work as well as to its ending! In this context, there is a story about a young priest who went to ask an older colleague how to write a good sermon. "A good sermon must have a good beginning and a good ending," the older man told him. "Then…it is a matter of bringing the beginning and the end as close to each other as possible!"

Lastly, and more anecdotally, it should be noted that this matter of beginning and end also applies to dress! Hair styling (or hats) and shoes are in fact the most important factors in our assessment, even unconscious, of a person's elegance. Someone with an ordinary suit, but with irreproachable shoes and haircut seems better dressed than someone with sumptuous clothes but with unattractive footwear or badly cut hair. Have fun checking this out!

We can also see from the allegory of the wax and hot water that many of our acts are not the result of a conscious and enlightened choice, based on extensive acquaintance with the subject. They are simply the result of our *habits*, or of our inertia, which make us mechanically follow the most obvious and well-worn paths, even when they are completely obsolete, inefficient or counterproductive.

For example: I am writing these words on the French "AZERTY" keyboard of my computer. Like the Swiss and most of the English, German and Italian "QWERTY" keyboards, it was designed at the time of the first mechanical typewriters. In those days the arrangement of the letters on the keyboard was intended to avoid two problems:

• on the one hand, that several keys might get stuck against each other when hit. Indeed, if one typed too fast, it could happen that a stem coming up could snag and block another coming down;

• on the other hand, that a key hit too forcefully might pierce the paper. We do not have equal strength in all our fingers, as can be seen for instance by the different print quality of letters typed on these old machines, sometimes lighter and sometimes darker.

To resolve these problems, the letters were spread over the keyboard in such a way as to *slow down* the typing as much as possible and to *limit* the use of the most agile and strongest fingers! This is why the letter "a", frequent in French, was designed to be under the little finger (the least agile) and one line above where the hands rest on the keyboard. The "q", which is much less used, is located immediately under the same finger. Conversely, the index and middle fingers, being the most agile, govern the letters "k", "y", "h", "g", "v" and "b", which are much less frequently used in the French language.

Well, in today's electronic age and with ultra-sensitive keyboards, *we are still writing on keyboards designed to slow typing down and use the least agile fingers!* This is in spite of the fact that on all computers we are now able to choose the keyboard we want at the click of a mouse. And yet a Frenchman, Marsan, has studied the occurrence of each letter of the alphabet in the French language and designed a keyboard to enable the fastest typing possible: this resulted in an improvement of up to 30% in the speed of professional typists.[17] But inertia and habit, in other words the *trace* im-

---

17. He also conceived his keyboard ergonomically, arranging the keys in a "V" so as to avoid the unnatural position of the hands that causes many wrist problems.

printed more than a century ago in the wax of our keyboards, together with our difficulty in challenging what appears to be established, means that we continue to mass-produce ultra-modern computers...with prehistoric keyboards.

In the same vein, people still sometimes say that it is not good manners to cut salad with a knife. Now the *raison d'être* of these "good manners" is simply the fact that old-fashioned knives were not made of stainless steel, and the vinegar in the salad dressing spoilt them. If we do not question the reasons for behavior inherited from the past, the principle of the impression made in the wax will impel us to perpetuate a whole host of behavior patterns and habits that have outlived their expiry date.

"Why don't you eat meat?" a friend of mine was asked one day.

"So why do you eat it?" was the teasing reply. Why indeed! The first questioner had never thought about his eating habits: by force of habit he simply continued what he had learned from his parents and family. Was this really the best food for him to be eating? Was it the tastiest? Did he know the advantages and disadvantages, the qualities and defects of the various nutritional choices one can make today? No. He simply followed the track imprinted in the family wax.

How many things do we do in this way, without ever really thinking about it? In our professional behavior, in our emotional reactions, our opinions, our beliefs, what part is played by an education that we reproduce mechanically without having ever consciously questioned it?

The wax represents the unconscious as well as the body, or matter. The hot water symbolizes consciousness, energy and the mind. Initially it is always the mind that starts by molding matter, it is the consciousness that orients thoughts and gestures, the programmer that writes the software.

Then habit takes over: the track is there, all we have to do from now on is follow it. This is fine as far as the good tendencies are concerned, the good habits and the behavior that we would like to continue. But what about all the habits that we didn't choose, that were there before us—in the family, in society—and that we didn't notice as they gradually established themselves in our daily lives, when we weren't looking, and which now govern us without our knowledge? One day, without us being aware of it, the body starts to dictate to the mind what it can or cannot do, the program limits the user, mechanical behavior supersedes conscious choice.

Take a look at the business world. Peter, for instance, creates a company. He is the hot water. It is he who decides what he wants to do, how he wants to regulate his company and what legal form he wants to give it. To begin with, it is he who molds the wax as he wishes, in accordance with his dreams and plans. But what often happens after a few years? The wax has hardened: the company is well established, bigger and more secure; it has become *entrenched* (an expressive adjective). And it is now the company itself that increasingly dictates to Peter what he can and cannot do. Creation has been replaced by production, administration, and management: these are now the main concerns. The business has its own life, its own metabolism and requirements. It becomes difficult for Peter, should he so wish, to make it change or evolve, to give it a new direction: it puts up a fierce resistance, it is not as malleable as it was at the start.

Indeed, a great deal of talent is required to keep a company alive and flexible, and to avoid the two extremes: continual change on the one hand, that neither the employees nor the clients can come to terms with, and on the other stagnation and petrification, which after a certain point make all change difficult and painful, not to say impossible.

When clay is left to dry, its form hardens; with too much kneading and moisture, it never takes shape and is useless. Life is a balance which needs to be constantly adjusted between body and mind, matter and energy, automatic unconscious actions and conscious choices. We need both the wax and the hot water.

The metaphor of this chapter is thus an invitation to discover what, in our own life, is the "wax" and what is the "hot water". In other words, to discover what comes from conscious choices that we still approve today, what has been unconsciously inherited from the past (family, social, religious), and finally, what we have introduced ourselves, but that no longer applies. To this end, we must periodically take a new look at our everyday environment. We must take nothing for granted. We must continue to marvel, wonder, be curious, question the evidence: "*Unlucky is the man who has not questioned everything, at least once in his life,*" says my favorite quote from Pascal. To question EVERYTHING, not just one or two things, such as the advice our parents give us (in adolescence), or what our boss or the opposing party tell us. Everything: our ideas, our beliefs, our knowledge, and our habits. We must allow no block of wax, no mold to continue to influence us without having questioned its origin, its value, its usefulness and its relevance.

It must be clear, however, that it is not a matter of change for the sake of change, nor of turning everything upside down for no reason. A lot of our habits exist for a reason, much of our behavior is appropriate and suitable. When this is the case, questioning them enables us to be aware of them, to make them truly our own, to turn them into deliberate and conscious choices rather than reflexes and mechanical habits. By taking possession of ourselves, we will be able one day to say that we are not just the result of a conditioning process to which we submitted more or less consciously, but the result of deliberate choices, made in full possession of our wits. This is a process that takes time—weeks, months, sometimes even years—but which is enriching and liberating. "*One cannot be free and ignorant,*" as Thomas Jefferson rightly observed. Freedom is not an acquired right, it is not given, it must be *conquered*. We are not free if we are unaware of the forces and conditionings that we have been subjected to and that continue to influence what we take for "free" choices. In symbolic terms, freedom is not strolling at will along existing paths, it is also the ability to carve out our own path.

It should also be noted that most of the great inventions are due to people who were able to marvel at things that everyone else regarded as normal or did not see (or had ceased to see). Coming back from a walk in the country, have you never removed small green or brown burrs from your socks without giving them any further thought? The man who took the time to reflect and to wonder why these little balls snagged on so firmly became the inventor of Velcro and made a fortune.

The danger of the wax lies in the trap of habit, the "automatic pilot". To avoid this we should choose consciously to modify certain habits from time to time, to opt for a new direction. Try buying a magazine you have never read before. Try cooking the food of a different country or just different food. Explore the beliefs of another culture, another religion. Exchange roles with your partner for a week. Eat with your left hand (or your right if you are left-handed). Fast for a day. Spend a month in chastity. Spend a day in silence. Play a game of basketball for the handicapped in a wheelchair. Get out of your ruts, out of the well-worn paths in the wax. Spread hot water over new ground. Make new tracks.

Perhaps you are one of those rarer types who tend to

get caught in the opposite trap, the hot water trap. This is the trap of some creative artists and inventors, of all who prefer ceaseless creation to getting stuck into something. As a result, they do not get to leave a lasting imprint on things, but are always inclined to explore new spaces, other possibilities, other expanses of virgin wax. If you are one of these, impose a fixed form on yourself. This might enable you to discover new dimensions of liberty and creativity. Practicing a regular discipline—martial arts, chair massage (Amma), yoga or meditation, chamber music, theater or choreography—can liberate our consciousness through the constraints it imposes. This is what happens in the case of the musician who plays the same pieces over and over again, but who each time breathes new life into the fixed form of the score. We only get bored when we do not know how to instill conscious and dynamic thought into an identical action that gets repeated many times over, but instead allow this action to dull our mind through monotony.

So, by paying attention at times to the content and at other times to the form, focusing now on the mind and now on matter, by alternating between creation and reproduction, consciousness and automation, everything turns into an opportunity for learning and integration, growth and fulfillment. And if you have left a fine impression in society, you might even end up at Madame Tussauds...as a waxwork.

The butterfly and the cocoon: Help that weakens and hardship that strengthens

When a caterpillar, having turned into a chrysalis, has almost completed its metamorphosis into a lepidopteran, it needs to pass one more test before it actually becomes a butterfly. It has to succeed in tearing the cocoon in which its metamorphosis has taken place, so as to free itself and take flight.

Whereas the caterpillar wove its cocoon slowly, bit by bit, the butterfly-to-be cannot free itself in the same gradual way. This time it must gather enough strength in its wings to break out of its silken casing in one go.

It is thanks to this ultimate test and the strength demanded of its young wings that the butterfly develops the muscle power it will need to fly.

Someone who is ignorant of this important fact and who thinks he is "helping" a butterfly to hatch by tearing the cocoon on its behalf will see an insect emerge that is totally incapable of flying. Because it has not been able to use the resistance of its silky prison, it has not been able to build up the strength needed to tear itself out of this straitjacket and launch itself into the sky. Ill-advised help can thus be harmful, even fatal.

This is a rich metaphor and it can be applied to many different situations. What can we discover from it? We learn, for example, that in life certain trials are indispensable for growth. They develop in us the strength to move on to the next stage. Conversely, if we try to resolve a trial for someone else, from the outside, by removing the obstacle, then instead of truly dealing with the problem, we in fact perpetuate it. So this turns out to be no solution. It also proves ineffective and generally ends up being counterproductive: instead of helping and liberating others, our ill-advised behavior can prevent them from developing, can weaken or even kill them.

Put like this, the idea behind the allegory may seem obvious. But look around you and you will see how determined people are, at every level, to "break the cocoons" of others, with the result that they perpetuate the problems they had intended to solve. Here are a few examples.

In his remarkable book entitled *Pourquoi sont-ils si pauvres?* [Why Are They So Poor?] (1992), which contains more than eighty synoptic tables, the Swiss ex-National Council Member Rudolf Strahm shows how ten years of aid to the Third World, costing billions of dollars, have ended by making these countries poorer, more dependent and more indebted than before. Of course one can put forward many explanations for this state of affairs: the corruption of one section of these countries' governments, the exorbitant cost of the debt, bad management of the aid, the sometimes ambiguous motives of the aid donors themselves. But beyond these various factors, it is above all the *nature* of the aid supplied (generally material or financial) and the *way* it is structured (by creating relationships of dependence) that need to be challenged, as several humanitarian organizations are in fact doing.

In the light of the butterfly allegory, we can see that certain changes, certain types of aid can only come *from within*. Thus, if we supply someone with something he lacks (or which may not yet have germinated in him), instead of helping him to acquire it by his own means we make him dependent and increase his incapacity. Of course, there are emergency situations which require immediate external aid, in the form of material goods, food or money. This is unquestionable. But apart from these cases, a truly disinterested aid—in other words one that is not trying to sell off surpluses or to keep a foreign economy under control—must aim to encourage others to acquire the capacity to help themselves.

A contrary example clearly illustrates this point. For as long as the government of the United States conducted a frontier war on the Native Americans, many of these tribes —destitute and decimated as they were—remained strong, expecting nothing from anybody and depending only on their own resources. As soon, however, as this government started to "help" them, putting an end to the fighting, giving them lands and basic means, these peoples began to weaken and perish (even though one always comes across occasional exceptions). I am deliberately simplifying here so as to emphasize the fundamental principle of the allegory: by supplying aid from the outside, one deprives others of the effort of seeking it within themselves, an effort that would strengthen them and enable them constantly to transcend themselves. This does not mean that we should therefore cease trying to assist or save others—a facile conclusion—but that our aid should support a person's effort to find his own inner resources, and not render that effort superfluous by substituting the easy way out and dependence on externals.

Another illustration of this principle is found in medicine. Many childhood diseases, from a simple cold to measles or whooping cough, for example, are tests for the child's organism that will then enable its immune system to develop and get stronger, as many doctors trained in Hippocratic, hygienic, homeopathic or naturopathic medicine know.

When we *fight* these diseases, as a certain type of medicine wrongly prescribes, we deprive a child of the chance to increase its immunity, we make it weak and dependent on external aids (medication, antibiotics, etc.). Indeed, certain well-informed doctors consider that one of the main causes for the increase in all sorts of allergies that we have witnessed over the last 20 years is precisely the over-medication of children, which prevents them from building up their immunity and makes them vulnerable to everything and anything.

If we really want to "help" a child affected by one of these childhood illnesses, we need instead to *accompany* the illness, making sure it does not get out of hand, and give the child's immune system the time to go through it and to come out of it better and stronger. *Give it time*: that is the key! By wanting to stop an illness in its tracks, so that the child does not miss school and we are not off work, we use methods that, although effective in the short term, create health problems later on, because the child's organism remains weak and fragile.

The same principle applies to fever, which is too often considered an enemy, whereas in fact it is the means the body uses to rid itself of pathogenic agents attacking it. As André Lwoff, a Nobel prize-winner at the Pasteur Institute, puts it: "A temperature is the best medicine. Beyond 103.1° Fahrenheit, most viruses are inhibited or destroyed." And André Passebecq, one of the founding fathers of naturopathy in France, adds that in a child whose hypothalamus has not been impaired by toxins (medication, vaccines), the higher the immune defenses, the higher the temperature can be allowed to go *without risking anything*, so that fighting off infection takes place robustly and swiftly. Passebecq stresses that "untreated fever leads rapidly to the recovery of health, without the risk of recurrence or complications".

By wanting to "rescue" a child from a fever, like the butterfly from its cocoon, we actually make it more dependent on medical assistance for the slightest illness. Conversely, the famous "sitz baths"—dipping a well-wrapped-up child's bottom into cold water for two or three minutes—which may seem like an assault on the organism, actually encourages a more vigorous and resistant immune system. The paradox implies therefore that certain forms of "aid" prove to be harmful while some seeming "assaults" prove to be salutary, although we must beware of generalizations and understand the process at work in both cases.

Two other areas in which we "rip cocoons open" on the assumption that we are doing the right thing are the upbringing of children (at home) and education (at school). As is often the case, over less than fifty years we have seen a complete swing of the pendulum in this domain. In the old days, children had no say either at home or at school. There was no interest, then, in hearing what children had to say. They were not the focus of attention, far from it. Parents and teachers had fewer qualms, and it was up to the child to follow, adapt, develop, or suffer the consequences.

Since all excesses attract their opposite, the work of psychologists and psychoanalysts led the next generation to see babies as people, take children's needs into account, show them greater attention—as subjects rather than as objects of education and pedagogy—and at the same time to tone down any form of constraint, authority or demand. From being not listened to in the past, children are now being over-listened to, which has given rise to this generation of "child-kings" who tyrannize their parents and teachers. Deprived of the cocoon of family and school, children seek to find replacement parents and an alternative framework in society and the state. As a result, it is society and the state against whom children now stage their awkward rebellion during the adolescent/chrysalis stage, a rebellion that goes on and on, since it cannot take place in normal conditions and on an appropriate scale.

Children have never had so many advantages, so much attention, so many possibilities of all kinds; they have never been so "helped". And yet, in conformity with the butterfly allegory, the result of all these external inputs is not what was expected. Without wanting to paint too black a picture—each period, since the beginning of time, has always found fault with the young—we must admit that illiteracy remains high, that the quality of spelling and writing has declined considerably, that the "80% success rate" on the Baccalauréat (French university entrance exams) is the result of a misleading drop in standards, that delinquency is on the rise among the young, and that moral principle is on the wane (words such as "virtue", "dignity", "honor" are disappearing from the vocabulary). In short, the internal pressure which promotes growth and development, anaesthetized by too much outside assistance, is becoming less and less. Incidentally, isn't there something that reflects this in the fashion the young have adopted nowadays for clothes that are many sizes too large for them? These clothes, that their bodies cannot fill, are a reflection of the functions and roles that await them but which they do not have enough inner substance to fulfill and assume, like a balloon that remains flaccid for lack of pressure to inflate it.

I repeat, I am not advocating a return to the past or a rejection of what science, technology and external methods can give all of us, including children. I simply want to say that content must take priority over form and precede it. The body must grow before the clothes, inner possibilities before external means. Things must happen "inside-out", must originate from within and then be externalized, taking on the form that corresponds to them in the outside world.

This was the understanding of a man from southern India, aged about sixty, whom I met ten years ago in France where he had come to negotiate the sale of some essential oils his company produced. This man had experienced the dramatic partition of India when he was seven. He had had to walk hundreds of miles with his parents, carrying a few basic possessions, to flee from the region that was to become Pakistan, because he and his family were Hindu. He started working when he was seven years old. Through willpower and perseverance he eventually formed his own company and ran it successfully. But he told me that when he died all his fortune would go to charity and that he would leave nothing to his children. I was surprised at this. "If they have the same abilities as me, they will not need my fortune," he told me, "they will make their own. And if they do not have my abilities, my fortune would only harm them, since they would not know how to put it to good use." In other words, he was giving his children the job of making their own made-to-measure clothes rather than leaving them his own, which might prove too large for them. Without taking this tale as a model to be slavishly imitated, I find that it has the merit of being coherent in a way that is consonant with the allegory of the butterfly. It gives priority to inner qualities—strength, courage, intelligence, leadership, love, resourcefulness, spirit of enterprise and many others—and sees material means and experiences as the concrete form or outer reflection of these qualities.

The fact that the man was a Hindu is surely not unrelated to this way of looking at things, because India, even though it is subject to various bad Western influences, remains a profoundly spiritual nation. With us, the very materialism of Western culture encourages everyone, in all fields, to prefer material, external solutions, rather than delving within ourselves, on the subtle level, for resources that only need to be actualized.

The tale of this Hindu is reminiscent, too, of those children's stories in which a king entrusts his son to a couple of peasants living on his land, so that he may be brought up ignorant of his royal origins and become acquainted with the earth, animals and humanity, catering for his own needs, so as to develop in him the qualities and knowledge that will later make him a king worthy of his responsibilities and duties.

We do not make a butterfly by sticking wings on a caterpillar, or a king by placing a crown on a child's head, or indeed a man by dressing a kid in adult clothes. We cannot give others what can only be the result of an inner and purely personal transformation. On the other hand, we can encourage this inner maturity, as we can water a seed to help it germinate.

The allegory of the butterfly also raises the question of suffering. Isn't it precisely in order to reduce the suffering of this insect, to liberate it more quickly, that we want to tear open the cocoon on its behalf? In a more general sense, when we want to help others, isn't it often with the aim of preventing their suffering, of making things easier for them? But is all suffering necessarily negative? Where is the borderline between painful effort, accepted and sought after in sports, for instance, and the threshold where suffering is judged to be unacceptable? There is obviously no set answer to this question.

What is certain, on the other hand, is that the "zero suffering" option is neither possible nor desirable. The same is true of suffering as of other things: there is good and bad suffering, necessary and pointless, indispensable and unacceptable. What distinguishes one from another is the *meaning* it has or does not have for the suffering person, or the meaning we are able, or unable, to attribute to it. Nietzsche said, "He who has a why to live can bear almost any how."

The suffering of the butterfly-to-be has a meaning, since

it is born of the effort that will enable it to fly: it is the price of its liberation, not only useful but essential. The suffering of a woman giving birth is the same, since it accompanies the giving of life,[18] just as the suffering of the baby being born contributes to the formation of its character when faced with hardship, as Grof demonstrated in his work on perinatal matrixes.[19] The same applies to the suffering of athletes who surpass their limits and break records. The extreme example was Christ, who went as far as giving a meaning to his martyrdom and death on the cross.

On the other hand, suffering atrociously under the dentist's drill is *a prori* meaningless, since anesthetics exist. To undergo mental torture for years as a result of the psychological effects of trauma or of having been abused as a child, when there are now various therapies that can set us free, makes no sense either. Deprived of meaning, a lesser pain is harder to bear than a pain which may be more intense but which does have a meaning.

Viktor E. Frankl, a survivor of the Nazi concentration camps and an author of some remarkable works, wrote: "To live is to suffer. To survive is to give a meaning to one's suffering." And he added: "Humanity seeks neither pleasure nor suffering, but a meaning to life." When meaning is absent, pleasure degrades and suffering destroys. The refusal

---

18. This does not mean that we should reject all means of attenuating pain, but just as an unbearable pain can traumatize mother and child, the absence of all feeling (which characterized the early years of the practice of epidural anaesthesia, for instance) can give a woman the feeling that her birth has been "stolen from her".

19. On this subject, see S. Grof: *Realms of the Human Unconscious* (Viking Press, New York, 1975) and *Beyond the Brain: Birth, Death, and Transcendence in Psychotherapy* (State University of New York Press, Albany, NY, 1985).

of almost any form of suffering (except in sport), like the frantic pursuit of pleasure, which characterizes contemporary society, can thus be seen as a reflection of the loss of meaning that many people acknowledge to be the case. Consequently, suffering is no longer evidence of the effort we make to transcend ourselves in a particular context; it is merely a useless, meaningless inconvenience that we must eliminate by external means: machines, medication, drugs.

To sum up, it is not a question of "suffering for suffering's sake", thereby creating a morbid cult of suffering, nor of condemning all suffering indiscriminately, and embracing a primal hedonism that is as unhealthy in the long run as the opposite extreme. It is a question of differentiating the suffering that enhances growth from that which destroys, as there is one fire—the sun—that warms us and ripens fruits, and another that burns everything it touches, reducing it to ashes.

If we really want to "help" others, we must inevitably ask ourselves this fundamental question about meaning: why is the other person suffering? What do they gain or lose by it? By suffering a little, are they getting stronger, more intelligent, more resistant, more tolerant, or are they not? Every parent, teacher, trainer or leader must one day face the question of the suffering of others and how to understand it and react to it. But, just as a child likes sweet things and hates the bitter things that adults appreciate, we need first to distil in ourselves the bitterness of suffering and taste the precious nectar extracted from it. Once this has occurred, we are able to let others perform the same inner alchemy, made possible by the fire of suffering, and keep them company rather than rushing at them with a fire extinguisher.

In law there exists an offense: "non-assistance to persons in danger". Thus, not to assist a suffering person—a seriously wounded person in an accident, for example—is punishable by law. But do we not witness at times the offense of "inappropriate assistance to persons not threatened"? This is what happens to the butterfly of the allegory, even though the offense does not feature in the penal code. The consequences of the first offense are obvious: an injured person might die or their condition might deteriorate substantially. The consequences of the second are less obvious since they do not affect the victim's body, but his *potential*: they do not affect his being, but his *becoming*, stifling from the outside what should emerge from within. Inappropriate assistance to persons not threatened is an offense against personal development, against growth and self-transcendence.

It was in this spirit that a great healer, concerned as much about the soul as the body of his patients, taught that before attempting to cure others, the true doctor must ensure that his treatment will enable the patient to go down the same path that his illness would have obliged him to follow. If this is lacking, mere physical cures, like the external liberation of the butterfly, would deprive the patient of the wings that would help him develop a full and entire understanding of his illness.

Clearly, the metaphor of the butterfly is full of wisdom. It stresses the primacy of the inside over the outside, of what is subtle, energetic or spiritual over what is material. *Inside-out*: allowing our inner potential to come out, encouraging our inner resources to function, rather than letting them atrophy through external action. It restores validity to our efforts in all areas, even to our sufferings, when they are useful, meaningful signs of self-transcendence and development. It invokes the principle of consent and emergence, as opposed to the ill-advised help that weakens or destroys what it seeks to rescue. A symbol to treasure, indeed!

The magnetic field and iron filings: Modifying the visible by acting on the invisible

Imagine a small folding Formica picnic table. A hidden magnet has been fixed under its surface. We then give someone a salt-cellar filled with black iron filings and ask them to sprinkle some on the table. They will see to their surprise that the tiny iron particles don't fall randomly on the table-top, but in a very ordered pattern which owes nothing to chance. The magnetic field, although it is invisible, in fact arranges the filings along the lines of force that unite its two poles.

Now imagine that this person, disappointed with the pattern thus formed, sweeps it away with the back of their hand and then sprinkles more filings, dyed blue this time, onto the table. Inevitably, the new iron filings form a pattern very similar to the previous one, but in blue this time.

If, on the other hand, someone separates or unites the poles of the magnet placed under the table, or if he places there two poles of the same polarity, instantly the iron filings, whatever color they are, will restructure in response to the underlying modification of the magnetic field.

This experiment, which has amazed many children at school or at home, is an excellent metaphor for phenomena that are encountered in many areas of human activity. What it teaches us is that a perfectly visible event can obey influences that are invisible but nonetheless real. When we do not take these subtle influences into account, the attempts we make to modify the visible part of the phenomenon are fruitless; the same patterns invariably recur. If we want to make a real change, we must deal with the deeper, invisible causes.[20]

The range of application of this metaphor is immense, so accustomed are we today to providing superficial solutions to fundamental problems, taking into account only the material, tangible, measurable part of the phenomena we are studying. Thus, whether in medicine, agriculture, education or politics, we strive to remedy the difficulties that arise by focusing on the symptoms, while neglecting the deep causes of which these are the visible reflection.

But the magnetic field and the iron filings exist first and foremost in each individual and that is where we should seek them out. The magnetic field within us is made up of all our beliefs: not only our conscious beliefs—religion, philosophy, the current of thought to which we are wedded—but also and above all our *a priori* baggage of values, preconceptions and implicit beliefs that we have developed while growing up (without verifying them) or that we have inherited from the milieu in which we have lived (family, social environment, country). Religious dogma is not the only thing we believe in. We believe in our fantasies, in what our fears suggest, in what others have told us about ourselves and the world. We believe in certain political ideas, in a given view of medicine, in cultural and social values, in what the newspapers say, in a multitude of things

---

20. I have used this metaphor in a previous work, *Modern Medicine: The New World Religion: How Beliefs Secretly Influence Medical Dogmas and Practices*, to explain the way in which modern medicine, since Pasteur, remains unwittingly influenced by a powerful religious current affecting its dogmas, practice and research.

that for the most part are unconscious, unless we have sought to be aware of them consciously.

Our "field of beliefs", as it could be called, powerfully and ceaselessly influences our way of being, our perceptions and also our way of thinking and loving. The "freedom of thought" so highly revered in our society is largely illusory at the present time. This illusion is typical of an epoch that makes a cult of the intellect and ignores, despite the discoveries of psychology and psychoanalysis (and of various spiritual traditions before them), all the subconscious and unconscious influences that operate on our so-called "free" thought. Just as the head could not survive independently of the body, our intellect does not think independently of what takes place in our heart (our emotions) and our body, both on the conscious and the unconscious level. In other words, our freedom of thought is in fact limited to our field of beliefs. This creates a space with borders that are both invisible and impassable, beyond which our thought can scarcely ever fly. In *Star Wars*, George Lucas brilliantly illustrated this relationship between the field of beliefs and freedom of thought: in his films, certain planets are surrounded by a magnetic shield, so that spacecraft can only operate within the invisible sphere that it forms, unless someone disables it. In the same way, no craft external to the planet and no intruder can penetrate this invisible but tangible border. This strikes me as a fine metaphor for that other sphere in which our thoughts evolve, a sphere defined by our beliefs and impermeable to ideas that are outside its field of influence.

If thought, according to poets, has wings, our field of beliefs is thought's cage and the strongest bars are our fears. There is no true freedom of thought without freedom of belief, in other words without an awareness of the beliefs that are operative in us. It is not necessarily a question of giving up our beliefs, but of having, at the very least, an objective view of the influence they exercise, so as not to remain their prisoners. To do this we must also work through the fears that give rise to this shield wall of beliefs within whose circle our thoughts go round and round, fears which prevent us from disabling it at will to explore new territories.

In the case of someone who has not updated the network of beliefs that his education has woven around him, thought is like a bird attached by a string on its leg, which can only move in a circumscribed and limited space. Even the most brilliant and highly trained minds are prone to these invisible influences. In science, in politics, in economics, everywhere, we find examples of great "thinkers", men and women of genius, whose works have nonetheless been biased, limited or distorted by their unconscious field of belief. The biographies of such personalities as Darwin, Mendel, Einstein, Freud, Pasteur and many others leave us in no doubt on this point. We cannot blame them, insofar as the training of scientists today is no more effective than it was in the past when it comes to teaching them to know themselves, so as to free their thought of these subterranean influences that interfere with their work.

If we want to make a real change in ourselves, we must deal with this underlying field and not only with what is on the surface. We can change our job, change our husband or wife, change countries, even change our religion, and still retain the same field of belief, which will soon reconstruct an identical copy of the situation from which we have fled or that we had hoped to change. A battered wife divorces and finds another husband who beats her. A harassed employee quits his job and joins another company where he gets harassed. A believer flees from the restrictions imposed by his religion and adopts others, more exotic but just as constricting, and so on. In each of these cases the iron filings change color, but never fail to fall into the same pattern as before. "We change and we change, but it is always the same," as the French saying goes. The expression reflects the degree to which changes affecting only the surface prove useless.

This shows us all the limitations of working only with the conscious mind, of dealing only with our thoughts: positive thinking, intellectual understanding of our behavior, affirmation. If our heart is not involved, if our emotions are not taken into account, if our blockages are not removed, if our fears survive deep down, if our beliefs remain unconscious, any change in us will be superficial and will not last. This is the reason why more and more new psychotherapies focus on all human dimensions—spiritual, intellectual, emotional and bodily—in order to produce change at a profound level in people's field of beliefs.

In the case of those who take the time to do this in-depth work, to deal with their own "field of beliefs", the surface changes tend to appear by themselves, as a natural consequence of what has started to happen deep down inside. When someone undergoes a profound transformation, they first change the relationship they have with themselves, then with those around them, relatives, friends and colleagues. Within a few years, sometimes sooner, people who have passed through an internal metamorphosis realize that their whole environment is spontaneously changing too: new professional opportunities, new lifestyle, new ways of relating to their spouse (or new spouse, according the path taken by each individual), without their having consciously decided or desired it.

More generally, the metaphor of the magnetic field and iron filings shows us that superficial changes last no longer than gold plate applied to a surface that is not prepared to receive it, and which ends up peeling off. When we impose a change, when we forcibly graft a new form onto a base that is not compatible with it, we will have at best a momentary illusion of having changed things, for as long as it takes this surface transformation to wear out, erode and disappear, leaving the base unchanged.

This, for instance, is what happens, according to André Giordan[21] of the Laboratoire de Didactique et d'Epistémologie des Sciences (LDES) in Geneva, when schools tack an external knowledge onto the preconceived ideas of children, without taking the time to identify and develop the latter. Giordan illustrates this with the concept most children have of the inside of the human body: most of them think that there is a tube from the throat which lower down divides in two to evacuate "poo" on one side and "pee" on the other. Since schools do not take this conception into account, teachers simply plaster it over with an intellectual varnish, explaining to children how the digestive system functions (esophagus, stomach, intestines, anus), which produces feces, then the renal system (kidneys, bladder, sexual organs), which produces urine. In his research Giordan shows precisely that this varnish lasts hardly any time at all. Thus we see adults, including members of hospital staff, who when asked to draw the interior of the human body start by drawing the esophagus, the stomach, the intestines...and then draw a division to evacuate urine in front and feces behind! The childhood concept, which was never identified, discussed or questioned, re-emerges years later through the cracks in the intellectual veneer. The teaching developed by André Giordan and his team starts instead

---

21. Teacher, college and lycée professor, research director at INRP and the CNRS in France, lecturer at Paris VII, André Giordan, now a professor at Geneva University, is the author of *L'enseignement scientifique à l'école maternelle* (Delagrave), *Une autre école pour nos enfants?* (Delagrave), and *Apprendre!* (Belin).

from the children's conceptions and goes on to develop them: knowledge is no longer tacked on from the outside, it is assimilated from within, as water is taken up by plants to develop their own leaves from what is made available to them.

Here is another example. Some decades ago, an ancient crucifix collapsed in a Peruvian church. This accident revealed that beneath the figure of Christ there was an Inca god. Later on, the same phenomenon was discovered behind several other crucifixes of the period. When they were forced to adopt a religion not their own, the inhabitants of ancient Peru hid their true beliefs under the forms that were imposed on them. They thus made a *literal* demonstration that this was no more than a superficial veneer, through which they continued to practice their ancestral religion. Beneath the Christ figure they continued to venerate their own Inca god. The "iron filings" of Christianity had changed nothing in the "Inca magnet", in other words in the field of beliefs which these people continued to maintain in their heart of hearts.

In a similar way, the attempts made in many countries to glue democracy onto populations that have lived for years under totalitarian regimes have often ended up with very mixed results, when these populations have not first made the inner adjustments to accommodate this form of government. The "democratic pattern"—the introduction of the political system—will only endure in a country where the way of thought and the social structure have been gradually evolving towards democracy. The turning away from democracy in Russia today, as I write these words, and the considerable difficulty encountered by the United States in bringing democracy to Iraq are typical examples of a clumsy attempt to reorganize superficially the political structure of a country without having first—and this requires a lot of time and effort—given the populations of these

countries the chance to bring their social and political awareness up to a level that corresponds to the democratic spirit. In biology we say that "the function creates the organ".
We would do well to respect this principle when we attempt to interfere in a country's social structure, and not
put democratic organs in place before its functional mech-
anism is able to cope with democracy.

In every sort of context, we often make the mistake of
thinking that it is enough to bombard others with arguments, objective facts, convincing proofs—in short to affirm our intellectual superiority—for them to change their
opinion and adopt the one we want them to. The reality is
altogether different. Beliefs are not intellectual: they depend much more on the emotional and irrational aspects
of ourselves. Reason, therefore, is rarely enough to weaken
them. True, we do sometimes get someone to change their
mind, when they are no longer able to answer all the arguments we throw at them. But for how long? As soon as we
turn our back they will revert to their initial beliefs, as well
as feeling anger or hatred towards us for having squashed
them with our cleverness.

Our ignorance of this process results in many mistakes
and much tactlessness and damage. In politics, for example,
some people imagine that superiority in argument is all
that is needed to convince supporters of extremist or po-
pulist parties to change sides. Worse still, they believe that
mockery, scorn and every form of judgmentalism are a
good way to persuade them to rally to another cause. The
result is quite the opposite: the more people are attacked,
the more they defend themselves and the stronger their
convictions become. Meanwhile, their aspirations, needs
and fears, the profound determining factors that make them
embrace that particular political program or ideology, are
not identified or taken into account. The result is that the

other parties do not propose any alternative which will meet their needs, dissipate their fears or provide an answer to their most urgent questions.

To sweep aside other people's political convictions without trying to understand what underlying principles they reflect is an inefficient strategy, as evidenced by the growing popularity of extreme right-wing parties, in spite of—or perhaps because of?—all the campaigns vilifying them. In contrast, the strength of a Gandhi, for instance, lay in taking the time to acquire a deep knowledge of the Indian people—their expectations, sufferings, aspirations, etc.—before formulating a political strategy that took these into account, whereas the other Indian political leaders made intellectual speeches totally divorced from the real concerns of their fellow citizens. Gandhi's approach, however, likewise had its limitations, for neither can non-violence be tacked onto the superficial behavior of an individual. It too must be the external reflection of a profound transformation of self, otherwise it will not last. In fact, we can extend this observation to certain so-called "non-violent" methods today that teach one what behavior to adopt and what formulas to use to communicate harmoniously with others, but do not deal with the hidden side of the individual from which his violence emanates. Hence, the paradoxical result that some people who follow these methods manifest incredible violence in their practice of non-violence!

A final example of this metaphor of the magnet and the iron filings in politics is provided by the United States. As shown by Michel Brugnon-Mordant in his book *L'Amérique totalitaire* [Totalitarian America], the messianic dynamism that presided over the creation of American society, and the mission this country still considers it has today, continue to influence the role that the United States intends to assume in the world. To ignore this religious background is to deprive ourselves of the possibility of understanding the mainspring of America's relationship with itself and the rest of the world. Thus, to expect that a new election, a new president or a new administration will result in a genuinely profound change in American politics is the same as to believe, in the terms of our metaphor, that replacing one layer of iron filings with another will result in a radically different pattern. The evidence shows us every day that this is not the case and that, at most, the only thing that changes is the political color of the pattern.

In a recent book on the differences between the two sexes, *Taking Sex Differences Seriously*, by Steven E. Rhoads,[22] I found another unexpected illustration of the principle of the magnet and the iron filings. The author explains that over a long period feminism, reacting to the excesses of the previous male-oriented society, spread the idea that male and female identity were mere social constructs and that there was nothing innate or biological about them. In other words, our sexual identity was the iron filings on the surface, not the magnet, our fundamental nature. According to the feminists it would therefore suffice to give exactly the same education to boys and girls for them to develop identically, androgynously. Similarly, those who supported these theories were convinced that by providing a child with an education deliberately oriented toward one sex, it was possible to develop in the child, whether it started out as a boy or as a girl, that particular sexual tendency, and to inhibit the other.

The facts and a large number of experiments, of which there is a vast inventory in Rhoads' book, have clearly established that the opposite is true, namely that from birth a child has a distinct male or female behavior, independent

---

22. Encounter Books, 2004.

of any education it receives. Rhoads cites the case of twins, one of whom, due to a medical error at the time of his circumcision, had to have his penis amputated and was finally castrated. His first name was feminized and he was given the typical education given to girls at the beginning of the 60s. However, the experiment was a resounding failure: the child continued to behave as a typical male; as soon as he could, he resumed his original first name and later got married (to a woman). Other experiments were attempted by some very feminist mothers, with the intention of bringing up their boys without exposing them to warlike toys (pistols, bows, rifles), and without stimulating their aggressiveness or their competitiveness, in the hope of bringing out their supposedly androgynous nature. These also failed and instead demonstrated the innateness of sexual characteristics. You cannot make a boy by sprinkling a girl with "male iron filings", symbolically speaking, any more than you can make a girl by forcing a boy to behave like a girl.[23]

In a general sense, this metaphor shows the dead-end that we come up against when we adopt a materialistic and superficial vision of the world. Such a vision leads us to ignore the deep or hidden determinants of many problems we try to deal with and, as a result, we apply solutions whose effect is likewise superficial and therefore ephemeral. Whether in relation to the great ecological challenges

23. This example—and this book—seem interesting to me because I think that the current attitude which consists in denying differences rather than learning to manage them and appreciating what they have to offer only leads to a dead end. It is as inefficient as the trick a school bus driver thought he had found. Each morning in the bus Blacks and Whites insulted each other: he made them get off the bus and explained to them that henceforth there were neither Blacks nor Whites, that they were all Blue—before telling them to get back on the bus, the dark Blues in the front and the light Blues in the back!

we face today, violence, hunger in the world, inequalities between North and South, or problems affecting education and schools, most of the solutions that are suggested aim to alter the pattern of the iron filings, to change the visible part of the problem. This generalization may seem hasty and exaggerated, but in fact it is not so. For behind the diversity and complexity of these problems, what is in question is the way the human psyche functions, in other words our way of loving and thinking, and in particular the relationship between our heart and our intellect, as well as between the unconscious and the conscious mind.

If we take a look around, all the objects that surround us, buildings, ornaments, a computer or a cup, a road or a telephone post, have all been *wanted* and *thought about* before they were made. This is a fact that we forget: we are surrounded by the material forms of *desires* and *thoughts*. Even our laws, our rights, our values, these more immaterial things that have so much influence on our individual and collective existence, were initially conceived by thought and nourished by sentiment. This means that the world crises and difficulties we face today, in whatever material forms they may manifest themselves in our lives, are primarily the result of a certain way of *thinking*, influenced consciously or otherwise by the emotional weight we give it.

Einstein said that the solution to a problem cannot come from the thought that created it. The same arrangement of the poles of a magnet always produces the same pattern in the filings. It is therefore not just new thought that we need today, but a new relationship between our thoughts and our feelings, between the conscious and the unconscious, between the two poles of our being that are the father and mother of our actions, of our material achievements.

This new relationship is characterized above all by our

awareness of the feminine dimension, hidden and subtle, that is always at work in our activities, whether or not we are conscious of it. The magnet is visible and so are the iron filings, but not the magnetic field. An idea can be expressed, its realization is perceptible: but the desire, the sentiments that enable the transition from an idea to its realization cannot be seen. Yet in the absence of these, the idea remains sterile, just as a seed without water will not germinate. No intellect, however brilliant, can give birth to something without the nourishing energy of the heart, of sentiment, passion and desire. The only projects that ever see the light of day are those that have found a heart to inhabit, where they can take shape, often wrapped at first in a protective and fertile darkness.

The pattern of the iron filings only changes if we alter the position of the magnet: if we arrange its poles nearer or further apart, if we do or don't place them in contact with the support on which the filings fall. In symbolic terms, therefore, real and profound changes in human achievements depend on the *relationship* between the heart and the intellect. The "war of the sexes", the eternal conflict between men and women, is merely the external reflection of the conflict between head and heart in each of us, which is itself reflected in everything we undertake externally. Our society today claims to be giving women more space: but what are we doing to encourage schools to develop not only the intellect but also the heart, our inner woman? What space do we give emotions and feelings at school, at work, everywhere? Just as, all too often, women only manage to survive in the modern world by adopting a masculine attitude, so our emotions and feelings are only admitted after being intellectually rationalized. Thus, we must achieve equality within ourselves first and foremost. This means balancing our intellect and our emotions. It also means acquiring a better knowledge of the relationships that exist within us between the conscious and the unconscious, between light and shade, between the soul and the body. As long as we continue to either ignore or despise any one of the components of each of these inner pairs, we will pay the price of the resulting imbalances both within and around ourselves, as each day makes clear.

Change, real and profound change, has nevertheless already begun and is growing. Personal development, psychotherapy, and the various means of communication increasingly assign to the heart the space and the role it deserves. Spirituality, whose multiple forms provide an antidote to groupthink, is arousing considerable interest, after having been mistakenly thrown away over a long period with the (holy?) bathwater of religion. A growing number of people are reading magazines or books, listening to broadcasts, attending lectures or taking courses about the "magnetic", the feminine, the heart, the hidden. And, unsurprisingly, we see that more often than not it is people who are working on their inner polarities—intellect/emotion, conscious/unconscious, spirit/body—who are also at the origin of new approaches to education, medicine, agriculture, science and other fields of human activity. Inner change is reflected and transmitted to the outside. Thus a new culture is gradually emerging, or more precisely several new cultures, as Paul H. Ray and Sherry Ruth Anderson have pointed out in their book *The Cultural Creatives: How 50 Million People Are Changing the World* (New York, Harmony Books, 2000). According to these authors, more than a quarter of the inhabitants of the Western world are involved in this evolution, which is constantly expanding. This time, it really is the magnet that has changed, first and in depth, and even if the old forms, made rigid by time, prove resistant to the new current running through them, nothing will ultimately prevent their gradual erosion and replacement by new structures, which accord with these profound changes.[24]

The allegory of the magnet and the iron filings thus provides a very interesting means for interpreting what is going on in and around us. It suggests that we should not dwell on the surface of things, on appearances, but go back to first causes; that we should deal with the deep determinants of whatever we want to change—within us and in the world—rather than wasting our time and energy on altering a form whose make-up is in any case subject to hidden influences.

In my view, one of the common denominators of human evolution that has existed for over a century is precisely the awareness of the hidden face of reality, unperceived by our senses, but whose role and influence are considerable. Freud, for instance, emphasized the notion of the unconscious, the hidden part of the psyche. In physics, Pierre and Marie Curie discovered radioactivity. The many waves that govern the function of so many familiar appliances—radio, television, cell phones, radar, sonar—were also discovered. The English biologist Rupert Sheldrake has posited the existence of "morphogenetic fields", of unknown nature and energy, to explain not only how the form peculiar to every living being is created (a question not resolved in biology), but to describe, over and above this, how certain learning processes in animals and human beings are transmitted from one individual to the whole species. Communication

---

24. …if not a global catastrophe that some indeed have prophesied. But the end of the world that they proclaim is perhaps only the end of a world. While waiting to see what the future does in fact have in store for us, it is preferable to nourish hopes of an optimistic scenario rather than to allow fear to paralyse us, thereby making it more likely that the worst will happen. In the final analysis, the future will be what we make of it.

specialists have discovered the importance of the non-verbal, what is said not in words, but with a look, a posture or an intonation. We have sent satellites to take pictures of the hidden face of the moon. Researchers have studied the olfactory influence of certain hormones at doses that are completely undetectable by our conscious perception, but which nonetheless determine our behavior.

The world, as we realize more and more every day, is not only matter, not only what we see or what our five senses allow us to perceive. We see only a small part of the entire spectrum of light, we hear only a little of the full spectrum of sounds; the mass of information that circulates in the universe every instant eludes our five senses, but it nevertheless plays a crucial role in the functioning of the visible world.

It could be that the physical world is merely the most dense and compacted part of a reality which we are only just beginning to explore, as the different spiritual traditions of five continents suggest. Like steam, which as it cools turns first into water and then into solid ice, matter is perhaps only the condensation of subtle energies—spirit, thought, feeling—that we are only just beginning to become familiar with.

In the past, we treated the world with physical force, building, sculpting, working with matter. Today, a few bits of information circulating on the Internet, invisible electrical impulses, can affect the life of millions of people. In future, a better knowledge of the creative and formative power of thought and feeling, as well as of man's spiritual faculties, will give rise to other even more spectacular developments. Ethical values, so difficult to respect in a world where everything appears separate, subject to chance and death, may come to be perceived as obvious facts when we develop an awareness of the unity of life, realize the existence of the energy which, like the magnetic field that survives after the iron filings have gone, survives the destruction of bodies and the ephemerality of forms.

The metaphor of the magnet, whose seemingly magic power fascinates even the tiniest children, invites us to explore the non-visible dimensions of reality and to learn how to create, on the subtle plane, what we would like to see manifested subsequently in the physical world.

The egg, the chick...and the omelet: From shell to skeleton

In an egg, the outside is hard (the shell) and the inside is soft (the yolk and the white). The hardness of the shell prevents the liquid content from spilling out before the chick has had time to develop within it.

Properly incubated, bathed in warmth, the egg allows its content gradually to form.

When the chick has fully developed inside the shell, we see that in its case the hardness is on the inside—the skeleton—and the softness on the outside—the flesh and the feathers.

Since it has now acquired its own form and its own inner solidity and no longer needs to be protected, the chick is able to break its shell and free itself of this confinement, which has become not only useless but suffocating.

By breaking its shell, the chick proves that it has completed its development and that it has interiorized in its skeleton the rigidity of the egg's exterior.

The transformation of the egg into a chick is an interesting metaphor for the transformations we go through as human beings. The shell of the egg is a very eloquent symbol of the structures inside which we grow up with as children, in other words the family, school, social, religious and political framework (or shackles) in which we develop. When we are young, this framework is necessary for us to structure ourselves, to build ourselves. We need these limits, in the same way that, like the egg, we need enough warmth—love, in symbolic terms—for the potential within us to develop.

This shell, however, is only useful for a while: in the end we are required to break it, for we have no more need of it when we have acquired our own inner strength. The religious and moral codes, for example, that we inherit in the course of our education should have the purpose of helping us to develop our own "moral or spiritual back-bone" so that we may, literally, be able to "stand up": once we have constructed this inner skeleton, we stand on our own two feet, and no longer need support or crutches. Our "uprightness" comes from being ourselves and no longer from our fear of the constraints imposed from the outside, laws, rules or moral codes.[25]

Individuals who have been able, within the family or social egg, to develop their own skeleton—their psychological and spiritual bone structure, their values—no longer need the shell imposed from outside and can easily break it. Henceforth, it is within themselves that they find the support and the strength to "stand up", to walk straight, not to fall over at the slightest opportunity (and to get up if necessary). Even if social structures collapse all around them, even in the midst of anarchy, chaos or war, even if they run no risk of being "caught" when they act wrongly, such people do not change their behavior, since it is dictated from within and is grounded in its own values. In fact, it is often the case, especially nowadays, that individuals who possess their own moral backbone have stronger and more

25. Viktor E. Frankl, already quoted above, had worked out during his time in the concentration camps a very simple classification of people that he applied both to his fellow inmates and to the guards of the camps: "There are those who know how to stand up (*anständig* in German) and those who do not."

resilient values than those that are current in their environment. Moreover, the people around them, at home or at work, tend to rely on such personalities—when they are not rebuking them for the firmness of their stance.

Indeed, we see that the best of social evolution has always been due to individuals who have possessed the inner strength enabling them to break the outer shells of their times, which had become obsolete, and to establish new social, political or professional models for the next generations, models which will be shattered in their turn by a new generation of "chicks".

As we know, not all of a hen's eggs will produce chicks. The shell may break before its content has had the time to develop, and this content spills, pours out and spreads. This is how we make omelets or fried eggs. The same thing happens on the human level, especially in collective phenomena. It happened, for example, in the case of the "social omelet" of May 1968 in France (the year of the student protests and general strike that almost brought down the government), and the liberation that followed. By breaking the too rigid social shell of the time, the leaders of this movement opened a breach through which poured not only those who represented new values, but a great many others as well whose inner development was not necessarily that advanced. More regrettably, this generation—in reaction to the struggle it had had to shatter the social, political and religious shell—was unable to provide a more suitable shell for the next generation. It thought that the latter could be exempted altogether and allowed to skip this stage, which it viewed only as a restriction without any formative function. The result was an "omelet generation", very difficult to channel, that went on to search desperately for an orientation and a structural framework, in the form of clashes with the police, or membership of sects or gangs.

After a generation of child-kings, or child-tyrants, as they were frequently called in magazine headlines, we are now witnessing a return to authority in the home and at school, accompanied by a still rather timid sense that it's OK to forbid things—timid, because forbidding things is associated with a questionable trend in politics (authority being seen as right-wing). Has the problem therefore been solved? This is by no means certain. History is often punctuated by swings of the pendulum between extreme positions, without the right balance being struck. The "social omelet" is one of these extremes. The other, symbolically speaking, is the rock-hard egg.

The explosion of May '68 was so powerful because the hardness of the social egg had by then reached death-inducing proportions. Indeed, a chick has a limited time in which to develop, mature, break its shell and emerge. If conditions are not favorable, if its development is incomplete, its shell becomes its coffin. It either never emerges or emerges stillborn. In the same way, educational, social and political systems do not necessarily fulfill the roles we have a right to expect of them. Some of them—totalitarian systems for example—aim rather to stifle any possibility of development, change or maturity. Others, although they may not be as pernicious, simply do not provide enough warmth to allow those who live within them to develop and mature. Others, lastly, have never been fertilized by the seed that programs the egg to develop and activates its potential to become a complete living being. Similarly, some societies are hermetically sealed to any new thinking, to the seeds of new ideas, to any spiritual breath that might revitalize their latent potential. These societies are spiritually sterile: they "function", they tick over, but they no longer create, no longer regenerate themselves, and, without even being aware of it, are very often already on their way out.

In a similar vein, it is to be regretted that in France the hostility to cults extends indiscriminately to everything that smacks of new ways of thinking in the fields of medicine, education, agriculture, economics or politics. In the past, the totalitarian countries of the ex-Soviet bloc demonized their dissidents, whose lucidity and courage were admired in the West. In France today, there are many movements composed of people who strive bravely to oppose groupthink, to remedy social fragmentation by initiating community projects or eco-villages, or try to take responsibility for their health and the education of their children—who behave, in short, like dissidents within the "system". Such movements are the object of discrimination, attacks or legal proceedings that are the trademarks of totalitarianism. Dangerous organizations do of course exist—cults in every sense of the word—but alongside these there are also some very varied initiatives (from utterly outlandish to exceedingly promising) that are unfortunately lumped together with the sectarian groups.

Just as the body, when afflicted by an auto-immune disease, can no longer distinguish between the harmful germs that attack it and its own "troops" and thus turns its immune defenses against itself, the French social body can no longer distinguish between cult-like organizations and ideas, and other organizations and concepts that are like a breath of fresh air from which the whole of society could benefit. The social egg closes in on itself and hardens, and—through fear of being "infiltrated" by a destructive germ—refuses any fertilization by new ways of thinking.

The transition from egg to chick is therefore not unconditionally assured and requires a whole combination of favorable factors: the state of the shell, the ambient temperature and the presence (or absence) of a seed are what determine whether the egg will or will not become the potential chick inside it.

Another important concept is contained in the metaphor of the egg and the chick: that of the alternation of the cycles of creation and destruction. If the shell is not destroyed, the chick is not born. And if, when they become adults, the new generation of hens and cocks do not in turn create new shells and do not fertilize them, there will not be another brood. Now, we have already observed that modern Western society rejects death and in general has a negative vision of destruction, which is nevertheless indispensable to all new creation. We see this not only in the ruthlessness we display towards people who are at the end of their lives, often with total disregard for quality of life (or simple humanity), but also in the fossilization of the past in which we engage on the grounds of archeology or of preserving our heritage, to a degree which has become pathological. I have no wish to erase the past and destroy everything that is ancient, far from it: humanity is rich in cultures and heritages, and it is important to preserve their remains—for as long as is reasonably possible. But is this what happens? Or are we in fact keeping moribund human creations on life-support machines?

Take the cathedral in Mexico City, for example. It is already virtually dead and is only kept standing by the use of extensive scaffolding. Is there any sense in this? Similarly, there is a huge outcry at every attempt to destroy any building which is the least bit old (not even ancient), in order to build something new. Fortunes are spent on preserving works from the inevitable ravages of time, works that have more than fulfilled their purpose, when the same money could be spent on new creations or to respond to real needs today, social, ecological or other. This attitude demonstrates a denial of aging, wear, and death, which paradoxically is itself an invitation to death, since it is a denial of the renewal, recycling, and regeneration that death inevitably brings and that is followed by new life.

To illustrate this I would like to cite something that happened about twenty years ago in Ladakh-Zanskar, a small Tibetan Buddhist land in northern India. A European foundation had discovered a magnificent and gigantic statue of the Buddha in a temple perched up in the mountains. The statue was very ancient, and serious deterioration had set in. In the opinion of members of the foundation, it needed urgent restoration. So they got the necessary funds together and sent them to the monastery concerned. When they received the funds, the monks hastened to destroy the ancient Buddha statue and set up a new one, of the same size and painted in the most garish colors! The notion of *impermanence* is in fact one of the most basic concepts in Buddhism: nothing in the material world remains eternally the same, everything changes, is transformed, dies and is reborn. Why keep an *old* statue? Why be attached to it? A new one fulfils exactly the same functions!

This story illustrates, almost caricatures, the differences in mentality between a materialistic society that is in denial of death, and a spiritual society that understands the eternal cycles of creation and destruction, life and death.

Beyond the issues of archeology and of preserving our heritage, our attitude to death also conditions the life and death of the social, political, economic or educational structures we set up. Obsessed as we are with *growth* and *development*, we no longer know how to destroy. Our society thus develops like a cancerous growth that goes on proliferating, to the detriment of the organism (in this case our natural and social environment). No death, no destruction, and no real regeneration either: we are content to re-vamp the form to make it look as though it's changed, like painting a chick on the shell of an egg to create the illusion of its birth.

We can therefore interpret several of the current crises —whether in national education, the growing lack of interest in politics or the various economic conflicts—in the light of our inability to break old shells so as to give birth to new forms. These are stifled in an egg that gets harder and harder. Perhaps, as in the case of food, we ought to set a consume-by-date for the systems we establish, so that once the period during which they are deemed useful has passed, we can more easily dismantle them and replace them with more suitable ones.

In fact, even though this would actually be a good solution, it is not indispensable, for things evolve in any case: in the long term nothing can stand in the way of change, because life is change and without it no life is possible. Our only real choice is the *manner* in which these changes are made: gently, in a constructive way, or else brutally, with breakage and violence. By refusing to accept the death and destruction of what has done its time, by opposing change and sticking to the status quo, we pave the way for brutal and violent transformations. We thus risk going again from one extreme to another, from one imbalance to another, alternating between the "omelet" and the "rock-hard egg", between laxity and rigid authoritarianism. Instead, we could work in tandem with the cycles of life and death which govern all things, anticipating, from the birth of a new system or creation, the wear and the end they will inevitably encounter. The metaphor of the egg is, indeed, a cyclical metaphor—egg, chick, hen, egg, chick, hen, etc.—which reminds us that life, at all levels, functions cyclically and not in linear fashion, which is how we are taught to see things under the influence of the rationalist mentality. History is not an ascending straight line, mathematically precise, starting from prehistory and reaching out to an ever more radiant future. It is a spiral with the ceaseless alternation of day and night, summer and winter, construction and destruction, growth and decline, war and peace, breathing in and breathing out. And thus, any attempt we make to suppress any one of the extremes of these polarities is doomed to failure.

Quinton's adder:
External environment
and inner strength

The biologist René Quinton (1867-1925), the father of seawater therapy and also of French civil aviation, the most decorated war hero in French history, was an unusual man in many ways.[26] Although, like Pasteur, he was not a doctor, nonetheless a remarkable intuition came to him one day that led him to use seawater for therapeutic purposes, in a form known as "Quinton plasma", which has saved the lives of hundreds of thousands of people.

Owing to the sometimes inexplicable waywardness of history, this man, who in his time was better known than Pasteur and was considered a benefactor of humanity, is almost completely forgotten today, and marine plasma is used only in veterinary medicine, even though it is unrivaled as a supporting therapy in human medicine.

This chapter focuses on Quinton's amazing intuition not on account of its medical applications alone, fascinating as these are in their own right, but also because, as a metaphor, it has so much to teach us.

While walking in the woods on an autumn day, René Quin-

---

26. One day perhaps a film producer may decide to make a film about this exceptional figure in French history. It would be an excellent subject.

ton came across an adder. As the temperature was rather cool for the time of year, the snake, which should already have been hibernating, was very drowsy and hardly moved. The scholar picked it up, brought it home and put it near the fireplace where a good fire was burning. After a few minutes, the adder, warmed by the hearth, recovered all its vitality and mobility. It even showed signs of becoming dangerous.

Seeing this, Quinton reflected as follows: "Life did not create the adder to be lethargic and drowsy: if it is so today, it is because it appeared at a time when the earth was permanently warm, thus allowing its vitality optimal expression."

On the basis of this first intuition, he formulated the following extraordinary theory of the evolution of zoological species on earth.

The very first forms of life appeared in the oceans at a temperature of around 109° F, when the earth, initially a ball of fire, had already cooled down considerably. As the earth continued to cool, the oceans also lost some degrees of heat. At the same time, the first species, which were in complete osmosis with their environment, cooled down with it. But life fought back against this decline by creating new living species capable of resisting the drop in temperature, preserving thereby the original, optimal conditions of life. Thus, these new species were no longer in total osmosis with their external environment: they possessed an *inner environment*, distinct from the external one, in which the original conditions of life were reproduced.

Over hundreds of thousands of years, as the oceans cooled down further, more species appeared of increasing complexity, capable of surviving at an increasingly different temperature from the external environment,[27] whereas previous

---

27. In fact the internal milieu enables us to preserve several of the original parameters, not only temperature. I am deliberately simplifying here.

species—such as the adder—were condemned to submit to the environmental deterioration and to live at a slower rate for part of the year.

Thus, the more the external environment degrades (entropy), losing its energy, the more life compensates for this degradation, interiorizing what has been lost externally and developing new faculties. As the external environment grows increasingly cooler, species learn to create their own heat. As the saline concentration of the oceans increases, living creatures increasingly preserve the original saline concentration within themselves. And at great depths, where light is lacking, certain species have evolved that are able to generate their own light.

Quinton, who was not a mystic, went as far as to argue that if one day the sun were to disappear, it would be because the living species had integrated it into themselves!

Whether this vision of things is valid or not in zoological terms,[28] it nonetheless gives us an interesting metaphor for certain types of human behavior, at the individual and social levels.

What was Quinton saying?

He stated that to begin with, at its birth (or its appear-

---

28. Generally speaking only Darwin's theory of evolution is taught, which is notoriously different from Quinton's. I have not found any fundamental criticism of Quinton's theory. However, it is certain that at the time it had the enormous "defect" of implying a form of intention in the successive appearance of the species, since according to Quinton the aim of life was to preserve the constants (salinity, temperature, etc.) of the original environment. We know that science, in reaction to religion, did everything to erase any notion of teleology in the evolution of the species. Today, however, many scientists, such as Michael Denton, author of *Evolution: A Theory in Crisis?* (Alder & Alder Publishers, 1986), bring solid scientific arguments to support the idea that evolution may obey a certain intentionality and not be the result of pure chance. The debate is still open.

ance), the living creature is in *osmosis* with its environment: the characteristics of this environment thus become its own. What happens then, when this environment degrades? Some creatures decline with it, unable to develop their own autonomy, while others resist the degradation and acquire an independence in relation to the conditions of the external environment. This they do by creating an *inner environment* for themselves which can cope with a more or less substantial difference from the one outside. In other words, faced with a decline in the conditions of life, certain species take an *evolutionary leap*, comparable to the healthy kick the nonsleepy frog gives to escape from a harmful environment.

What happens when we transpose this principle to human existence?

Like aquatic species, we swim from birth in a human environment which possesses certain characteristics, where different family, religious, relational, political and cultural values prevail. Most of these we absorb not through education or through explicit teaching, but indirectly, subconsciously, by osmosis with the environment in which we live. Without our being aware of it, our mentality is thus formed in the more or less faithful image of our surrounding context. "Our" values, "our" beliefs, "our" conception of life are thus largely an osmotic reflection of those in which we have bathed since childhood.

"Unlucky is the man who has not questioned everything, at least once in his life," said Pascal, as already quoted above. Indeed, it is this questioning that alone enables a person to sift through everything that they have passively absorbed in childhood, so as to keep on one side what will then be consciously *ours,* and reject what we do not want. Until this sorting through has taken place, values and beliefs appear to be part of us which, until proved otherwise, are in fact primarily circumstantial. If we had been born into a differ-

ent family, country, or culture, the values, beliefs, and vision of the world we call "ours" would undoubtedly be quite different.

In the absence of such self-scrutiny, a change of environment may prove revealing. This can happen in two ways:
- one suddenly enters another environment,
  by traveling, for instance, in other cultures
  and countries;
- or the environment within which we have grown up
  itself goes through a change, which can be rapid
  (wars, economic depression) or gradual
  (progressive decline or evolution, as in the case
  of the frog).

The adolescent son of a friend of mine, for example, went to spend a year living with a family in the United States. After being thrown into this new environment, he says that a few months later he noticed that he had lost the craze for hygiene which characterizes his own family, and had developed a less obsessive relationship with cleanliness; on the other hand, he remained as keen as ever on punctuality, in contrast to the host family. This stay abroad helped him to start to distinguish between what truly belonged to him, among the things handed down by his parents and country of origin, and the behavior patterns and habits he had adopted by osmosis, but which can disappear in a new family or social environment.

In a similar way, wars can reveal the presence or absence of an *inner environment* in those who live through them: some people turn out to be heroes and oppose the savagery and cowardice that surround them; others tune in to the general mood, while others are torn between their aspirations and what they are actually able to achieve. No one can really know how they would act under such circumstances, unless they have already experienced this trial by fire in a similar situation.

However, as we saw with the frog, it is the slow and gradual changes that really test the strength and constancy of our values and beliefs. When it is brutally thrown into hot water, the frog immediately kicks itself out and escapes with its life. It is easy to react to something violently opposed to what we believe in. It is more difficult to discern something that strays only slightly from the line we have chosen; the risk is that this may become the new norm, and that then another insignificant deviation may in turn create another new norm even further removed from the first, and so on. The accumulation of these minor deviations results in a life as different from the one we led at first, as the adder's life is different when it goes from a hot climate, where it is active all year round, to a temperate climate where it is forced to hibernate for half the time.

These various metaphors, from different angles and offering complementary illuminations, are talking basically about the same things: how to remain aware, how to develop, affirm and preserve our values, how to resist what goes contrary to the direction we have chosen, how to draw strength from adverse circumstances.

In the light of this metaphor, our own times strike me as especially interesting. Indeed, many people call them "apocalyptic", not in the sense of catastrophe, as this term is frequently understood, but in the original sense of "revelatory".

Over more than a century, as Nietzsche prophesied in *Twilight of the Gods*, many collective frameworks and terms of reference have gradually disappeared, one after another. Many taboos and prohibitions have been cast aside. Not a year goes by in which the limits of research, morality and ethics are not pushed further back (genetic manipulations, cloning, stem cell research, single-sex marriages and adoptions, the patenting of living organisms, and, on television, violence, sex and the extremes of reality TV).

The social, human, economic, professional, political, spiritual and relational environment in which we are bathed
(not to mention the environment itself) is changing at an
increasing rate, perceptible from one decade to the next,
and which may soon be perceptible from one year to the
next. These changes inevitably affect each one of us: the
question is *how?*

It is worthwhile asking oneself: what does this evolution
reveal to me about myself? As the social climate gets colder
for lack of human warmth, am I, like Quinton's adder, losing
warmth along with the environment, or am I more like the
warm-blooded animals, capable of preserving my own inner
fire? In a human environment characterized by spiritual entropy and darkness, am I sinking into the night without even
being aware of it, or do I have my own inner light, my own
spiritual life, independent of the external context?

By day, nobody sees the stars; we need the night to see
them shine. Similarly, it is in the cold of winter that one can
best distinguish warm-blooded from cold-blooded animals,
which are condemned to slow down and hibernate. Again, in
a social climate that retains a certain intellectual and spiritual light as well as a degree of warmth—social ties, love—one
cannot distinguish the people whose light and warmth come
from within from those who, like phosphorus or heating
bricks, merely give back what they have absorbed from their
environment. It is only when the collective values and the
social climate deteriorate that we can discern those people
who continue of themselves to give out light and warmth.

Hence the need to ask the question: when external conditions change, what still remains exclusively my own? What
can I claim to be truly *mine*: what values, what positions,
what opinions or points of view? Do I possess an inner personal, independent environment? Am I more of a reptile,
like the adder, or more of a mammal?

At the collective level, the good news is that the number of people capable of resisting this degradation of the external context is actually much greater than one might think if one listened only to the main media channels. At any rate, this is what emerged from a study carried out by two American sociologists over a long period (nearly 14 years) and involving a very large sample of the population (about 100,000 people). This study was issued under the title *The Cultural Creatives: How 50 Million People Are Changing the World* by Ray and Anderson, mentioned above.

Cultural creatives are ordinary people like you and me, but who have chosen partial retreat from the cultural environment in order to devote themselves to something more in accord with their values: they have chosen—like you perhaps—another way of treating themselves, or of educating their children, or a more exacting way of consuming (fair trade, organic produce), or a new lifestyle, healthier food habits, etc. In a word, they have made a *personal choice* that runs counter to the dominant values, at least in one area of their lives, instead of following a general trend that does not suit them.

The term *cultural creatives* is interesting and revealing. It suggests that the people who resist the cultural degradation around them do so not only on an individual basis, but in order to reconstitute, even on a small scale (a community, a company, a village), new cultures—a plurality that is precious in these times of groupthink. This is an important point. Indeed, while Quinton demonstrated that life is capable of resisting the increasing entropy of the environment, more recent discoveries in the field of ecology go further and indicate that living species can not only resist the evolution of the environment in which they live, but can in turn *transform* it. For example, the astonishing stability of the mineral composition of the sea—considering what gets poured into it on a daily basis in the form of rain, silt, and all kinds of waste—is due to the animal and vegetable species (fish, crustaceans, algae, etc.) that live in it and work constantly to maintain this balance on which they depend. In other words, these species modify their external environment, the sea, in accordance with their needs. In a similar way, we know that the same kind of reciprocity exists between the plants and the climate of certain regions: on one side, the climate determines which plants grow in a given place, on the other these plants influence the weather that develops over their heads.

Human beings have the same ability. Not only can they resist social changes that are contrary to their aspirations, they can also change their social environment to conform more closely to the latter. This is precisely what the *cultural creatives* are trying to do, whether or not they have heard the term, and whether or not they are aware that they are implementing this process of individual resistance and collective transformation. The originality of their approach, in relation to other approaches whose tendency is political, is that it derives primarily from an internal change which then seeks to reproduce itself in the external world.

In the United States, cultural creatives already represent nearly one quarter of the adult population (44 million people, according to the study). Even though such a study has not been carried out in Europe, many indications lead us to believe that the percentage of cultural creatives there is similar. A quarter of the population is a considerable figure, even if it has not (yet) given rise to social or political structures capable of directly changing the course of events (compare this to the much lower electoral scores achieved by certain extremist parties that everyone worries about).

In symbolic terms, then, the cultural creatives are a warm-blooded species that on the one hand strives, in spite of the spiritual entropy of the environment, to preserve an inner environment with its own morality and values—in other words a certain inner fire—and on the other to reproduce these inner qualities in the social environment, so as to change the external world. There is nothing, however, that distinguishes them externally from other people: they are not grouped under any single banner, they are not uniform in their choices, even though they act from a similar impulse, a similar desire to oppose the decline. Most of them do not even have any idea that they are known under such a name. This fact—the absence of any external defining characteristics—is food for thought. Up until now, the concept of "mutation" has been associated with the *external*, visible transformation of a species, as described in the Darwinian view of evolution. It might be that with human beings the time has come for *internal mutations*. These do not affect their physical appearance or physiology, but first and foremost their vision of things, their way of thinking and loving, the relationships they develop with themselves, with others and with the whole universe. It might also be the case that this mutation, if we can call it such, needs to be accomplished individually, each person affecting his or her own, and that it cannot be automatically passed onto descendants, though the right education would undoubtedly encourage it. And this, finally, may be the only real solution to the problems we are currently facing. The implementation of new laws, new technologies, new medicines—all products of the way of thinking that created these problems in the first place—cannot in itself profoundly or sustainably change anything. Inner change—a new way of thinking, loving and acting—must precede and inspire the development of methods and solutions that are truly new and able to address the root causes of our current problems.

So far, we have focused mainly on what the metaphor of Quinton's adder has to teach us about the capacity of life —whether an individual or a group—to oppose the deterioration of its environment. In a certain sense, we have stressed the exception that proves the rule, when the rule is no longer acceptable. We can also look at this metaphor from the opposite viewpoint. Rather than showing how one black sheep can extricate itself from a flock that is charging dangerously toward a precipice, we can reflect on the power of the flock, of the environment, of the atmosphere, the importance of the context, the power of numbers. In fact, the first thing Quinton's theory shows is the natural tendency of the individual to be in osmosis with his environment, to adopt its qualities and/or its defects. This was what the first forms of life that developed in the oceans did. It is also what most children do in the family, religious, social and cultural environment in which they grow up. To begin with, osmosis is the rule, individualism the exception.

In view of this, we ought to pay much more attention to the type of atmosphere or environment we create—or that we passively allow to develop—within our society, at school, in the family, in the different contexts in which we evolve. If we create swamps, should we be surprised when bloodthirsty mosquitoes emerge from them? If we allow storm clouds to form, why should we be surprised when destructive thunderbolts crash down? Since the rule stipulates that as a given environment degrades, the *majority* of the individuals living in it tends to degrade with it, priority should be given to the quality of the surroundings, of the general atmosphere, of the framework of life.

We have all experienced the importance of atmosphere, of the context. If someone who lives in the country goes to spend a day in Paris, for instance, their behavior is immediately transformed under the effect of the stress that characterizes a big city: they are on their guard, their muscles tense up, they are more careful about their valuable belongings (wallet, jewels, purse). Similarly, anyone who spends a few days in a monastery, sharing the life of the monks, will certainly feel the effects of such an environment with its alternate sequence of chants, prayer, silence and conscious work. In this context, suddenly they no longer feel the same; they might even become aware of another dimension, latent in them, that cannot manifest itself in terms of their usual lifestyle. It is a fact that some surroundings awaken the finest dispositions latent in us, while others can dangerously titillate the beast that is hidden deep within.

This phenomenon is often most evident in children, since their capacity to resist the influences of the environment only develops as they grow older. Thus, a child who is labeled "difficult", "restless", or "disruptive" in one context, such as school, can be found to be very pleasant, cooperative and easy to live with in a different context, such as extra-curricular activities, a different school, etc.

Our individualistic culture has its advantages and its disadvantages. Among the latter we may count a very reduced capacity to create and preserve healthy and stimulating contexts in the way we live, study and work. We emphasize the individual without concern for the general context in which he develops and which influences him considerably.

Social fragmentation is one of the main characteristics of life in modern Western society and is represented by ghastly surroundings in which everyone strives to get ahead like explorers in a jungle. While this may actually develop in some people a certain inner strength, it certainly does not help to improve the quality of life in general.

At a time when "personal development" is all the rage, it is worth remembering that healthy and balanced individuals, who have taken the time to work on themselves and develop, do not exist in isolation; they evolve in a social environment which can in fact prove to be not only sick in itself, but noxious for those who live in it. True, as we saw above, one can fight against contamination by one's environment, but this resistance has a price. It requires great energy and effort which as a result cannot be used for anything else. Alongside personal development, "collective development" or "social development" should also be considered and implemented. In this way an environment would be created that responds to the needs of an expanded individuality, while at the same time *encouraging* the fulfillment of others ("encouraging", because the individual is always free to accept or reject the influences brought to bear, even when these are positive).

What I want to stress here is simply that it is important to work both on the individual level, which I mainly talk about in this book, and on the collective level. Since not everyone has the same capacity to turn adverse conditions into a medium for strength and growth, it is also important to try and improve the environment in which we live, the general context, so as to encourage the development of everyone. The metaphor of Quinton's adder should not be understood as an elitist view of evolution, leaving behind all those who cannot emancipate themselves from difficult external conditions. It also suggests that those who have acted as pioneers, in being the first to accomplish an inner mutation, are then responsible for the creation of better external conditions so as to encourage the evolution of others.

We have come a long way with this metaphor of Quinton's adder. First, we saw that the environment exerts a natural influence on those living in it, who tend to be in osmosis with it. The second stage showed that it is possible to resist the degradation of this environment, to acquire autonomy and become independent. We then went beyond or, rather, extended Quinton's ideas in the light of more recent discoveries, showing how human beings, empowered by the transformations they have brought about in themselves in order to break free from their environment, can subsequently modify this environment in conformity with their values and for the benefit of others.

"Whatever does not kill me makes me stronger," said Nietzsche. What I lack externally, I develop within myself, was Quinton's way of putting it. What I have developed within myself, I communicate to those around me so that everyone may profit from it, as demonstrated historically by such figures as Jesus, Gandhi or Mandela. To be influenced and then to influence others; to use individual fulfillment for collective enrichment; to pull oneself up above the rest and then to haul them up too; this continual give-and-take between the individual and the community is what gives evolution its alternations and rhythm.

Conclusion:
Are we cooked or not?

We have reached the end of our seven-stage "Journey into the world of Allegory". I hope it has given you a taste for metaphors and a glimpse of the lessons we can learn from natural phenomena, so long as we take the time to observe them. Nature is a great book: everything in it is symbolic, everything speaks to those who learn bit by bit how to decipher its language, and to distinguish the correspondences between all things. Where some people see only chance and chaos, others perceive order and meaning. Phenomena that to some seem distinct, separate, unrelated, can reveal themselves to us as closely linked, connected and interdependent. Symbols and metaphors help us to re-establish a link, to reconnect—consciously in this case—with the world around us.

It is no accident that today there is a strong renewal of interest in *rituals*. Books, articles, workshops are proliferating on this subject, whether for personal, family or professional use. Rituals are, indeed, founded on symbols and connections: the candle we light symbolizes the flame of the spirit that we want to awaken in ourselves; the objects we bury represent the elements of our past that we wish to discard; the tree we plant evokes a new creation, a new departure. Each gesture we make in the course of a ritual corresponds to something within us. The more we become aware that everything is linked, tied, connected, the more we are naturally inclined to use these links and, by way of rituals, to enable a transition, mark an important moment, mourn a loss, or celebrate a happy event.

The first stage of our journey is therefore consciousness or awareness. Consciousness today is very much of the mind, very analytical and narcissistic—like Narcissus, modern man is absorbed in a consciousness of self arising from his capacity for *reflection*. We need to replace this with a consciousness more intuitive, sensitive and profound, that does not focus on appearances, that goes beyond the reflective surface of the mental mirror and arrives at a richer, more complete perception of the world. Narcissus contemplated his reflection in the water and ended by falling in and drowning: this is another fine metaphor to conclude with. Did you know that Narcissus is at the origin of the terms "narcosis" or "narcotics", that which induces sleep, illusion, the sleep of death—narcissi are planted on tombs? Consciousness, therefore, must choose to wake rather than sleep, must say no to mindlessness and drowsiness, must prefer life to fake paradises and virtual universes. We are thereby choosing to open ourselves up to others, to create a connection, whereas so many gadgets today tend to isolate us from one another in artificial bubbles. Narcissus must die, yes, but he dies to a limited, unconscious existence. Yes, he must pass through his reflection, break the mirror of the water, but in order to arrive at a new dimension, at a consciousness greater than the mere consciousness of self. Human beings acquired self-consciousness and differentiated themselves from the animal world through their cortex, their mind. But this individualization is not an end in itself, any more than is the isolation of the chrysalis in its cocoon: it is the prelude to a new participation in the world, once the cocoon is torn and the mind is superseded. The different forms of yoga, prayer, meditation and contemplation free up other possibilities within us, activate other perceptions and awaken latent functions which enable us to transcend our ego.

So, in the final analysis, are we already half cooked? Probably not yet, but the fire is burning nicely under the pot. Are we going to end up like the frog or free ourselves like the butterfly? Are we dying stifled in the egg or are we going to break the shell, strengthened by our inner conquests? Will we make an evolutionary leap or will we, like the adder, remain spiritual reptiles?

Although this choice is primarily up to each individual, it will also be influenced by the number of those among us who have opted for evolution rather than for death-inducing entropy. It is very likely that after a certain number of individuals have been transformed (the critical mass), change will be easier for all who come after, although it will continue to depend on each individual's conscious decision. As we learned from the Chinese bamboo, it could be that the invisible changes that many people are trying to bring about today may lead, when the time is ripe, to an external transformation that is both startling and swift. This is my constant hope, as well as my dearest wish.

About the author

Born and raised in Geneva, Switzerland, Olivier Clerc presently lives in Southern Burgundy, France, with his three sons. He works as a writer, translator and editorial consultant, specializing in spirituality, shamanism, health, personal development and human relationships.

Olivier has crossed paths with many famous authors and teachers whose books he has translated into French, and with whom he often trained. Among them are Charles Rojzman, founder of Transformation Social Therapy, Marshall Rosenberg, founder of the Center for Nonviolent Communication, Don Miguel Ruiz, Dr Deepak Chopra, and many others.

He started his carreer as an author at the age of twenty (his first book, which turned out to be a success, was on lucid dreaming). He is the author of six books, including *Modern Medicine: The New World Religion*, published in the U.S. by Personhood Press (2004). For more information please visit his website, www.olivierclerc.com.